MW01248613

BRAND SHADOW

Understanding and Overcoming Corporate Toxicity

Brand Shadow
Understanding and Overcoming Corporate Toxicity
A Guide for Navigating Corporate Trauma and Toxic Cultures

Stephanie Crain

©2024 All Rights Reserved. No portion of this book may be reproduced, stored in a retrieval system, or transmitted in any form or by any means-electronic, mechanical, photocopy, recording, scanning, or other-except for brief quotations in critical reviews or articles without the prior permission of the author.

Published by Game Changer Publishing

Paperback ISBN: 978-1-963793-53-6
Hardcover ISBN: 978-1-963793-54-3
Digital: ISBN: 978-1-963793-55-0

www.GameChangerPublishing.com

DEDICATIONS

I'd like to dedicate this book to:

My five best bosses and two of my worst. You helped me
learn a lot about myself, and for that, I am grateful.

Ed, you see my light. You always have.

Kelly. Just cuz.

Read This First

Just to say thank you for buying and reading my book, download your FREE **Reflection Journal and Action Guide** to *Brand Shadow*, no strings attached!

For Free Gifts, Scan the QR Code:

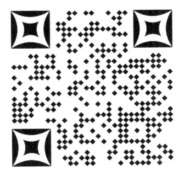

Brand Shadow
Understanding and Overcoming Corporate Toxicity

A Guide for Navigating Corporate Trauma and Toxic Cultures

Stephanie Crain

www.GameChangerPublishing.com

FOREWORD

As a leader building teams, I searched for the "X" factor, that person who brings a vibrant, strong and unpredictable dynamic to a team. Not an easy thing to put in a job qualification, yet when I saw it, I felt it. Twenty years ago, Stephanie was the "X" factor for a team I was building.

As I write this foreword, 20 years later, as a former boss, I reflect back over those years and see all the seeds Stephanie was planting and sowing. Twenty years ago, I may have thought she was the "X" factor for my team, but I had no idea how enormous her "X" factor was; I was merely scratching its surface. Now, it makes perfect sense why Stephanie was an incredible team player, designer, marketer, leader, and coach through those 20 years. She observes, she listens, she learns, she sees. So much wisdom to share.

I am lucky; I can and have tapped into her wisdom. I did through the years because I wanted her read on a business environment or situation, both formally and informally. I'm retired, so now I find myself asking her a lot of business questions so I can hear her stories. All those years of observing, listening, learning, seeing, sharing to anyone who listens.

People enter and leave our lives daily. Some people's impact or influence on us is immediate and others' impact or influence on us is so subtle that we don't fully realize it until another part of our journey. I hired a graphic designer 20 years ago. I got a lifetime friend.

- Janet Gossage

TABLE OF CONTENTS

PREFACE

America is extremely stressed out. According to the CDC, one in five adults lives with some form of mental illness, and over 80% of the workforce suffers from work-related stress.[1] Our systems aren't supporting our most basic needs, whether we're looking at healthcare, community support, or even family systems. We are under significant pressure, and we don't have the mental and emotional support we need to deal with it. What's more, we haven't been taught how to provide it for ourselves. On top of this – or perhaps at the root – is the fact that we live in a capitalistic system that requires us to go to work and earn money so that we can support our lives. In itself, this is not a bad thing. It only becomes a problem when the system you depend on to live is also depleting the very essence of your life – your health and spirit. When the very system meant to sustain you simultaneously drains your well-being, you're in a difficult position.

There are a lot of work systems in America, but the main framework for most business is the corporate system. Corporate systems are present in various work environments beyond the typical office setting, and many of these systems do not support our health needs. Over time, this has created a

---

[1] CDC. "About Mental Health." *CDC.gov*, 28 Apr. 2023, www.cdc.gov/mentalhealth/learn/index.htm#:~:text=More%20than%201%20in%205.; Boyd, Danielle. "Workplace Stress." The American Institute of Stress, 2022, www.stress.org/workplace-stress#:~:text=83%25%20of%20US%20workers%20suffer

1

pattern of what I call Corporate Toxic Stress Disorder, or CTSD. People generally understand that "work-life" balance is critical, but we have to negotiate that against the concept that our time equals money, and often more money for someone else. The time that we spend in our lives is valuable and must be valued through that lens, yet many of us are conditioned to devalue ourselves. The more deeply we become misaligned in this way, the harder it becomes to thrive, and the more we are diminished.

In *The Myth of Normal*, Dr. Gabor Maté discusses the difference between "big T" traumas and "little T" traumas.[2] Big T traumas are what we usually tend to associate with the word "trauma," such as war, assault, or natural disaster. Little T traumas, in contrast, refer to everyday stressors and emotional experiences that may not seem significant in isolation but can accumulate over time to impact mental health and well-being. These can include experiences such as relationship issues, minor accidents, workplace stress, or ongoing emotional neglect. While little T traumas are easy to overlook, their impact can be significant. They impact us mentally, physically, and emotionally, and they build up over time.

My premise is that Corporate America has created a system of micro-traumas that we have all been conditioned to accept as normal, in the way that Dr. Maté explains. In organizations, this becomes internalized over time as a *Brand Shadow*, or an aspect of the culture or business that is actively ignored or avoided while creating damage to the business. I believe that many people who are working in that system are traumatized, and the data shows that many people have left corporate systems because of trauma.[3] A recent study of "The Great Resignation" by *MIT Sloan Management Review* showed that

---

[2] Maté, Gabor, and Daniel Maté. *The Myth of Normal: Trauma, Illness, and Healing in a Toxic Culture.* New York, Penguin Publishing Group, 2022.

[3] "Toxic Workplace Cultures Cost Companies Billions." DaMar Staffing Solutions of Indianapolis, 8 Feb. 2023, www.damarstaff.com/blog-posting/2023/2/8/toxic-workplace-cultures-cost-companies-billions#:~:text=One%20in%20five%20Americans%20has.

toxic culture was ten times more influential than compensation in employee attrition, or churn.[4]

My Trauma-Informed Past

I have a trauma-informed past that has nothing to do with Corporate America. I was born with medical anomalies, which required me to have a multitude of surgeries from a very early age. During my childhood, while having several surgeries, I experienced many micro-traumas, but I had a significant trauma when I was ten years old. I woke up during surgery and saw myself physically cut open at my belly. That traumatic experience wasn't analyzed until well into my adulthood, and at the age of thirty-six, I was diagnosed with C-PTSD, or Complex Post-Traumatic Stress Disorder. Before the diagnosis, I went through a period of my life where I struggled, not knowing what was causing the struggle, and I had to seek my own path of healing. I did that and began healing in many different ways from a very early age, first through therapy, and then by incorporating mindfulness practices and other healing tools. I was learning more about myself so that I could gain personal agency over my own body and medical care. As I went through those processes of healing, it allowed me to broaden my perspective and look at the system of medical care in a particular way. I saw the way that I fit into it as an individual and what my personal agency was within the medical system. This experience gave me more perspective when I looked at other aspects of the world. My diagnosis of C-PTSD allowed me to explore my trauma with precision and learn even more about how trauma impacts our behaviors and our health, both short and long-term.

---

[4] Sull, Donald, et al. "Toxic Culture Is Driving the Great Resignation." *MIT Sloan Management Review*, 11 Jan. 2022, sloanreview.mit.edu/article/toxic-culture-is-driving-the-great-resignation/.

My Journey into Corporate Spaces

I came into the corporate world via a non-traditional route for a variety of reasons, primarily related to my medical challenges and the issues that resulted from them. I wasn't able to pursue a traditional degree or have the typical college experience, so I entered the corporate world like many corporate misfits do: through sales. In sales, it really is about the bottom line and the ability to get the work done: the ability to create relationships and connect with the client. A good salesperson can sell themselves first, proving their capacity for the job. This ability can remove many barriers in the corporate world. I was a smart salesperson and understood my job very well. I was working in technology, and I came into the corporate world in the '90s, which was a really interesting time for that industry. Technology was an extremely male-dominated space at that time, and I was okay with that. I've often joked that I was raised as a "firstborn son" by my dad. He was very corporate, masculine, and disciplined, and significantly influenced my life. He taught me a lot of skills that I didn't necessarily recognize, understand, or, in some cases, even appreciate until later in my life. Some of those skills were how to not shrink, how to be strong, and how to hold my own space. He taught me that my words and actions needed to align. He taught me that I could do anything that I set my mind to.

These and other skills in communication and creativity gave me a propensity towards leadership. Others recognized it in me, sometimes before I could see it in myself. Over time, as I grew and developed in my career, I leaned into leadership and the challenges and opportunities that came with it. I find the experience of leading people immensely rewarding: the opportunity to solve problems, build consensus, learn, be accountable, and add real value to people's lives. To me, leading is connecting action to purpose and propelling those around you towards their highest potential.

This book is intended for people who see the possibilities inside of problems and the opportunities that come from change. They are ready to illuminate the shadows that have created so much distress and waste in corporate spaces. It begins with the individual claiming empowerment. Ultimately, I believe that we have reached a point of innovation in Corporate America, a time when change can and should occur. This book is for you if:

- You are a manager who is tired of surviving in a toxic environment and ready to thrive instead.

- You're an executive leader who is responsible for your company culture and ethos and wants to leave a legacy that inspires others.

- You're part of a leadership team that wants to avoid common pitfalls and dated approaches while growing your business.

- You survived Corporate Toxic Stress Disorder and want to know what comes next.

I hope that by sharing my experiences and perspective, along with current data and immediate actions you can take in your life, this book will help us move beyond toxicity and into new realms of possibilities. My goal is to illuminate the *Brand Shadow* so we can innovate towards a higher purpose, where values are aligned and acted upon for the betterment of organizations and the people within them. If you want to play along with the book and explore some of your own corporate shadows, have your journal ready. There will be reflections to ponder and actions to be taken and explored. I wish you the best on your journey.

– Stephanie, aka Corporate Mystic

INTRODUCTION

| Shadow Stories

In many ways, these are *my shadow* stories. Each of these experiences is true as told, but intentionally vague regarding the specific details because that isn't what's important. What is important is that these were pivotal moments of self-awareness. These were points in my career where my personal boundaries or values were challenged and the ways in which I responded to them reflect my emotional growth. All of these occurred early in my career, as I was growing, learning, and developing as a professional and these and other experiences like them taught me a lot. Through these experiences, I learned how I showed up, the energy I projected, the things that triggered me most, and the values I held close. I also learned how to claim my voice, challenge the status quo, that being different and tenacious was often an asset, and that sometimes quiet observation was the best approach.

Reading these might make you think that I feel embittered or cynical about the corporate world, or as one friend said "I didn't realize things could be so bad." In fact, the opposite is true. I feel like I was given witness to all of my experiences for the purpose of perspective. I have spoken to people from all over the world who have shared their own shadow experiences, and I do not feel unique—instead, I see patterns. I also see possibilities. These shadow stories and a few others throughout the book are snapshots, but in no way do they represent the fullness of my career. Over the years I have worked for and with many wonderful people in great organizations. I learned a lot from them as well. Mostly that there are wonderful people and great companies out there and if that is true, then there can be more. Now, onto the Shadow Stories.

Playing with the Big Boys

When I first came into corporate technology, I was working in network integration services as an inside sales rep supporting outside sales reps. At some point, I had become knowledgeable and successful enough that I was making more sales than the senior reps I was supporting. They were all male, and it was a male-dominated environment. At the time, there were maybe four women working in the company and about 20 or 30 men, mostly engineers. I wanted to transition into outside sales. I had clients who were requesting it, so I asked to do that. In some ways, I demanded it, because I felt like I had earned it. There was resistance to this request, and it came primarily from the top, but I was persistent. Finally, I was invited to an executive sales team meeting, and it was clear that the owner of the company was unhappy that I was there. I did have some champions on my side, and that's partly why I was in the meeting. I had colleagues who saw the work that I was doing, really believed in it, and wanted me to rise up, but the owner of the company was not one of those people.

The owner opened the meeting by welcoming me to the table and asking if I was ready to "play with the big boys." My immediate response was, "I thought I was sitting at a table with men, not boys, but you're the boss." He was not amused, but neither was I. Later, I found out that the owner had been sued for sexual harassment and discrimination by other women who had left the organization before me. This was entirely consistent with my experience in that environment. I wasn't there very long before I moved on to another technology company with a similar environment but a much better culture overall.

Stalker Client, Betrayal Boss

Many of my clients had been telling me about a new tech company that they liked working with. They liked the owners and thought the company had a great vibe, and they wanted me to move over to that company. They didn't like the company I was working with, but they liked me as a sales rep. So, one night, I contacted the owner. I looked up his phone number and called him at his home. It was a bold move, but it paid off.

He answered, and I said, "Hi, my name is Stephanie, and my clients are telling me that I should be working for you. So, can you tell me why?" We had a conversation, and he hired me on that call that night. I started working for this company and was one of five sales reps. Up to that point, they had never made more than $1 million in revenue as an organization in a year. I believe they had reached $998,000 the year preceding the year that I started, so they were right at that threshold. I was their first sales rep to do a million-dollar month. We ended my first year there at around $8 million. I brought in nearly half of that revenue while working on 100% commission.

I did exceptional work for them, made a lot of money, and it caused me a great amount of stress. Sales and I did not go well together, and no amount of money could fix it. As good as I was at that job, I always had health issues. I had constant insomnia – the worst in my whole life, before or since. I even broke out in hives on my hands. I was always stressed out, and I placed a lot of pressure on myself to be exceptional, not just in sales but, more importantly (to me), in relationships.

Then I got a client who was just a bad client. I mean, really, there is no other way to describe it. They were just a bad client. They hired us because their current tech guy was getting ready to leave – not on amicable terms. They needed to fire him, but they were worried that he was nefarious, so they hired us to back-end the situation so that they would be more protected. It didn't work. Turns out he was nefarious and undetected; he put a virus in their system that launched about eight months after he left the company. They had waited too long to address a toxic issue, and the damage was done before we were ever involved. Instead of replacing him, they decided to outsource their needs to our company. The real problem was that they were just never a good customer. They didn't pay their bills, their environment was filthy, and they didn't take care of their equipment. They were a horrible service company because they were constantly calling us for ridiculous needs. Worse, they treated our engineers badly, and no one wanted to support them. At some point, I wanted to fire them as a client. I didn't think that they were worth the effort.

The relationship with them kept getting more and more tenuous. I knew that the owners of the company had both been going through divorces, and they partied excessively, so they were often hungover or high when we met. I hated meeting with them because they were so erratic. They didn't treat me with a lot of respect either, and over time, they started to harass me. The harassment escalated to the point where I received screaming, raging phone calls in the middle of the night, waking both me and my husband, and also included receiving very cryptic emails. The emails came at all hours of the day or night and would be filled with quotes from Shakespeare, typically about revenge or death, combined with abusive rants. Essentially, these felt like death threats, and the energy was very hostile. I took all this to my boss, and he told me he would take care of it. He told me that he agreed it was problematic, and I believed him. I had no reason not to believe him – I was his top salesperson. Then I came to work the next day, and as I was walking past the conference room, I noticed that my boss was sitting in there with the two owners. Honestly, it terrified me.

The situation had been hostile enough that I really didn't want to be in their presence. So, to have them in my office space without warning was jarring. I didn't know why they were there, and I didn't know what they were talking about, but at a glance, it didn't look tense. Everyone was smiling, and my boss was laughing. I went to my desk and sat down. A few minutes later, my boss came out of the conference room and called to one of our junior sales reps. She had been on board for just a few weeks, and I was her executive mentor. It was her first sales position; she had never worked in sales and had never worked in technology. He called her into the conference room and assigned her the account, which was upsetting to me for a multitude of reasons. Aside from the betrayal and what I thought was a shitty business decision, I was actually fearful for her as well. I felt like he put her in a position that was unsafe, which I considered unacceptable.

I had worked hard for this company and believed in it. It was like a family, and I felt deeply betrayed. I met with my Betrayal Boss and confronted him about his decision. I told him that, more than anything, after having learned so much and being so loyal to the business, I was disappointed in him as a person, not just as my boss. His response was to start crying and apologize. He said he felt terrible for what he did, and he didn't really have an excuse for it. This grown man was sitting in front of me, bawling because he knew what he did was wrong. But he had made a decision and, for him, a value-based judgment. He made a choice, and I had to as well, because it simply did not align with my values. So, I quit the job. He begged me not to – I was still a high earner.

I quit anyway, and then I turned around and took another position in the company. At that time, I knew I didn't want to stay in sales; it wasn't going to be good for me. It was not good for my health, and after that situation, I had really lost my spirit for it. I passionately wanted to do something creative, and I thought that I would do well in marketing. The business leaders had the autonomy to hire within their own departments, and there was a position open as a front-desk receptionist. So, I took the job as the company's front-desk assistant and enrolled myself in graphic design school.

It was an interesting response to the situation. I did it for a few reasons. The main one was that I didn't feel like I deserved to have to leave. I hadn't done anything wrong, and I also felt like it was important to hold my ground in that space and ask them to respect me no matter what. I don't know if they did or not. I mean, my Betrayal Boss seemed extremely frustrated that he had to walk in and look at my smiling face every day. I didn't mind their discomfort at all. I enjoyed being a receptionist and had fun with my role. Plus, I had the time to study graphic design and move on, which I did.

The Elevator Ride

My first real graphic design job was a transitional role for me. Even though I had worked in executive professional roles and managed people, I've always been someone who will take steps backward to move forward. I climb peaks, drop down to examine new details, then start climbing another peak. I've always felt like a corporate explorer in that way. Most of my education has come through corporate experiences. I approached each job as a chance to advance my knowledge and experience, and I tried to learn everything I could about the industries and the environments I worked in. Not just my job but the jobs around me, understanding the processes and the way the departments work together. When I first got hired as a graphic designer, it was in a traditional, conservative corporate environment, dissimilar to technology spaces, and markedly different from startup spaces that I had worked in. This environment was a "button-up shirt-and-tie environment." Without question, everybody in the company had a degree. Most people had MBAs, and many of my colleagues had double degrees. I felt like an imposter who would be discovered at any moment. When I took on that role, I told my friends that I got my first grown-up job. From day one, I can honestly say that I never fit into this environment. The only reason I even got an interview was because I knew somebody who knew somebody. I was always a fish out of water in that space, not because I wasn't smart, but because I was different.

However, I valued and appreciated the opportunity to be there, and I learned a lot of valuable life lessons and professional skills during my time there.

One thing I will never forget was my very first day. I arrived, and the front desk person greeted me, telling me where I needed to go, which was up to the top floor to get my new desk assignment. I took the elevator alone; I was the only person there. It climbed to the second or third floor, then stopped. The doors opened up, and I was facing a conference room with a large group of people filing out, laughing and talking loudly. It was clear that they were The Executives. The energy of ego and authority coming out of the conference room was palpable. They filed right into the elevator, all of them. I felt myself shrinking as I pressed back against the elevator wall, disappearing into this crowd of close-knit strangers.

They were mostly men (but not all of them), and they all knew each other. The energy felt almost playful, if not slightly aggressive. They were jostling and shouting, basically making fun of one particular guy because they were frustrated with him. I heard one of the men shout out, "If I've got to go to sexual harassment training one more time because of you!" and then burst out laughing. I was standing silently, listening to and absorbing this information of what was going on here. The senior executives had just come out of harassment training, and apparently, it was this one guy's fault. From what they were saying, it had happened more than once. What's more, it was no big deal because "that bitch got fired." I was absorbing all this information as I was riding up the elevator, thinking, *Where am I working? Like, what is this?* I'm not a prude. I had only ever worked in primarily male-dominated environments. People would not call me an introvert at all. I show up strong – I mean, Aries rising strong. I show up with a lot of fire. But in this space, at that moment, none of that energy was there. I just wanted to hide. I didn't want anybody to see me. I didn't want these people to see me at all.

Later that day, my friend who recommended me took me around to the different floors, showed me which departments worked where, and introduced me to various people that I might be working with. We came down to this lower floor, and I understood that this was the department where that guy worked. I don't think that my friend was expecting to see him at all. Most of the executives were typically traveling, but they were obviously all there that day for their training. He happened to come out of his office and just sort of run right into us, and my friend introduced us. He shook my hand, but while doing so, he looked at my friend, who said that I was replacing the previous graphic designer. Without even looking at me, he scowled at my friend, "Oh, that bitch. I hope you're better than that." I was dumbstruck, and it's not like me to be speechless. I usually match energy, but that was strong negative energy, and I didn't want to drop that low. I let go of his hand and smiled.

"Wow. It's great to meet you." What else could I say?

Just Speak Slowly

I was working as an executive in marketing, supporting multiple business lines. I was responsible for managing all aspects of marketing for the business units I supported, including event-related marketing. One day, I was scheduled to meet with an executive in one of the business units to review plans for an upcoming workshop he was heading up. He and I were peers (based on rank), but he often came across as arrogant and disrespectful to the marketing team. It wasn't uncommon for him to reschedule meetings at the last minute, fail to follow up on action items, or just not show up at all. He would give excuses about how busy he was, but other, busier executives were capable of being responsive and respectful, so his justifications were hard to take seriously. It was also obvious that he treated different people in different ways, currying favor with senior management while generally disregarding people below his rank. I had raised concerns about the challenges and extra work he was creating for our team, but the head of the business unit didn't see it as an issue. It was an issue for my team, and I had received enough feedback that I decided to work with him directly. My marketing managers were frustrated too.

On this particular day, I went to his office, where our meeting was scheduled, punctual and on time. When I walked in, he was sitting in his office, scrolling on his computer. He quickly turned his chair toward me and grabbed a closed folder sitting in front of him. He opened it and said, "You need to meet with my assistant. Something came up." I explained that he had scheduled this meeting and that he was also the only person who had the details we needed to create a campaign for his event. He shrugged and said his assistant could handle it, looking down into his suddenly important folder. He was notorious for blowing off deadlines and disrespecting my team and I debated saying more, but I knew it wasn't worth it. Besides, he was so difficult to work with that I felt like I would accomplish more without him, even though his assistant had very little of the details I needed. Since we were scheduled to meet in his office, we would be forced to meet at her cubicle desk in the hallway. I was frustrated because, besides lacking the space to meet properly, it was disruptive to the people around us to have a meeting of that nature. I noticed there was an empty office with just a desk in it nearby and I suggested we move our chairs and meet in there. The assistant and I gathered our items, moved locations, and began our meeting.

Since the point of the meeting was to develop an event marketing strategy, which was something we did frequently, I began creating the strategy. I documented the few details the assistant did know and worked with her collaboratively, making executive decisions based on past experiences as we worked. At some point, he overhears our discussion and comes out of his office to interject. I had outlined some detail that he disagreed with and he needed to let me know. He suddenly appears in the doorway of the office. He wasn't a particularly large guy, but he stretched his arms up the sides of the doorframe, filling the space. As he attempted to loom over us, his energy was hostile and dismissive. He raised his voice immediately, demanding information that wasn't readily available or relevant and insisting that I wasn't doing my job properly. Since I had already made it clear that for me to do my job properly, he needed to do his job too, I found this somewhat amusing and annoying all at once.

My response was to remain calm. I reminded him that this was originally his meeting and also his decision to be dismissive and not attend. When he did that, he also absconded his authority over that time slot by effectively canceling his meeting. I was working on my own time and would have been well within my right to reschedule when he said he wouldn't meet with me. Since he was expected to participate but chose not to, I set a firm boundary that this type of interruption was inappropriate and disruptive. I told him I would gladly reschedule with him, and we could follow up on the items he was referencing, as we had initially intended. He continued to try and intimidate, raising his voice louder while making more demands. His assistant appeared to be wilting before my eyes, and I wondered how often she experienced this. Even so, the louder he spoke, the calmer and slower I responded.

Finally, I calmly stated, "You can keep shouting louder, and I will only respond s-l-o-w-e-r. Please let us finish our meeting." I watched as his face transformed from pink to a deep red. He opened his mouth again, his words increasing in volume, and I interrupted him. With deliberate slowness, I said, "I may not have been clear. If. You. Talk… LOUDER… I. Will. Only. T-a-l-k s-l-o-w-e-r."

While I could see how much my response upset him, he was also disarmed. He stared at me for a moment, silent and breathing—he appeared to be collecting his thoughts. We had reached an impasse, and his go-to strategy for intimidation and dismissal wasn't working. He looked at his assistant and said something to her about unrelated work he needed completed, then as abruptly as he showed up, he turned around and went back to his office. Staying calm while acknowledging his behavior helped to diminish his energy. More importantly, I honored my values, stood up for myself, and modeled that behavior for someone else to see.

I met with him the next day and addressed the situation one-to-one. We had a reasonably productive meeting and moved on. While we were never friends, our working relationship became more productive and that was what mattered. Once I established a clear boundary, he never expressed that type of behavior to me again.

Witnessing Corporate Trauma

I have witnessed corporate trauma in several different environments. For me, even witnessing corporate trauma is traumatizing. I would even put some of these situations under the category of big T trauma. In one environment I worked in, I was a senior-level executive. I managed a small team at that time, with maybe five or six people. I had an office in an executive suite space, so there was an executive office on each side of mine. One day, I heard a literal scream of rage come out of the office to my right. As I stepped out of my office to see what was happening, I saw the back of my colleague's head as he stormed down the hall. I followed him. He was a professional friend, somebody I sometimes had lunch with and who had once come to dinner at my home to meet my family. I knew enough about him to know he had some personal things going on, but I had no idea what was going on at that moment. He was a kind, friendly person, and this behavior felt very out of character. As I followed him, other people peered out of their offices and cubicles to see what was happening. He stormed into another colleague's office, somebody else who was also a professional friend, and physically attacked him. He blindsided my other colleague and screamed obscenities as he physically grabbed at him. The person who was attacked happened to be standing up at his whiteboard at the time and was completely caught off guard by this co-worker who was in an absolutely violent, hostile rage.

It was extremely frightening for everyone there. Other male colleagues came in quickly and were able to separate them. The reason for the outburst was work-related, and it wasn't personal. They had worked together as friendly colleagues for months without any problems. I believe the deeper issue had to do with many things: the pressure of the environment that we were in, the pressure of the work that was expected at the time, and industry pressures. More importantly, I think that this individual was dealing with his own personal pressures and mental health stress, and, as was expected in most environments, he was hiding it. He was trying to keep everything secret out of fear that people would see him as weak, or because he feared getting fired or stigmatized. Ultimately, all of that energy and emotion boiled over and created what ended up being a highly unfortunate scenario that felt traumatizing to many people.

I've seen many emotional breakdowns in corporate spaces. I've had people come into my office and burst into tears. I have walked into people's offices and burst into tears. I have seen tempers flare in conference rooms and heard people scream at each other through closed doors. I have seen men cry nearly as much as I have seen women cry. There's a myth that women are the only people who are emotionally reactive in corporate spaces. But in my personal experience, I would say it's fairly equal. It has more to do with how we are judging these emotions and reactions. They might be expressed differently, but the emotions that are coming up serve the same functions. People are reacting to unreasonable demands and expectations in environments that are sometimes so toxic that, on an energetic level, you feel sick from the moment you walk in. Our bodies and our central nervous systems can really only handle so much stress. Many micro-traumas that happen in corporate spaces show up as emotional exhaustion and emotional breakdown.

I've seen people, and even owners, do unethical, illegal things. Early in my career, a company I worked for was investigated for internal crimes – someone had been suspected of stealing from the company. It was very serious, and what made it worse was that the senior director was accusing a close friend of mine. He was actually my neighbor and had given me a referral for the job. I genuinely believed he wasn't responsible for what they accused him of. They called the police, and we were all interviewed at the police station. It's my only experience of a situation like that, and I remember being terrified. The police were intimidating and wanted me to say that I knew something. But I didn't know anything and kept saying so. After about an hour, they let me go. I ran out to my husband, who was waiting for me in the car, and I burst into tears.

A few weeks later, the director and her husband were arrested for embezzlement and stealing laptops and computers. They closed the office, and we all lost our jobs. My friend was vindicated, but it was a terrible experience. Up to that point, it seemed like a great job, and I was learning a lot, but I was young. There was a lot more to learn. I've also witnessed behavior that I find nauseating: open racism, blatant misogyny, and emotional abuse. For me, those situations are intolerable. The people working in organizations with this energy, especially the people with the least influence, are usually impacted in the worst ways.

For me, when something crosses an ethical boundary, I have to speak up. I have done so many times, and then I leave. I can't support it, and I don't want to be a participant. I've seen abusive people get promoted and celebrated, and even celebrated for their abuse. I have always had a saying that when something becomes a running joke, it's a distraction from an ugly truth. I feel like that kind of energy shows up often in toxic environments with certain types of people. I also think that there's a cycle of trauma similar to cycles in family systems.

In a dysfunctional company, that cycle of trauma self-perpetuates because leadership is driving the culture, and culture is driving the business. In the context of leadership driving the culture, they're going to model and create what people see as successful. The people who come into the environment are going to try to reflect that behavior or match it to impress the leader. If you have a leader who leads with fear, or they're authoritarian without empathy, it can be very damaging and ultimately counterproductive.

This is an example of how toxic companies often mirror dysfunctional families, where the dysfunction happens in cycles. In a similar way to how dysfunctional families teach the next generation how to be dysfunctional, toxic leaders often develop and promote what serves their needs best. It usually takes somebody to break that cycle by calling it out or creating some level of hyper-awareness that reveals undeniable truth. In dysfunctional families, that person is often referred to as "the black sheep." In corporations, they might be called "whistleblowers."

Usually, the black sheep is the person who is expressing the family dysfunction externally. In corporate environments, whistleblowers or those who speak up and complain will often get called out as disruptive because they are calling out the dysfunction. I don't necessarily judge authoritarianism in and of itself. Like most things, I believe it can be balanced. I think you can have authoritative energy mixed with empathy. I think that that's possible and sometimes quite necessary. But in toxic situations, abusive authoritarians will use intimidation to keep others silent.

Several factors made it easy for me to recognize these patterns in organizations: my personal experience with trauma; my dysfunctional or unconscious patterns, which were closely related to traumatic experiences; and my personal healing process, which enabled me to learn about and understand trauma on a personal level, as well as the patterns in my own life. Not every environment I worked in has been toxic. I've worked in some great environments that were very uplifting and which allowed me to thrive. Again, it makes it more obvious, I think, to see the trauma patterns when you have something to compare it against that isn't traumatic.

Overcoming CTSD is a worthwhile endeavor. It's time for us to acknowledge corporate shadows, the things that companies have historically hidden behind branding, marketing campaigns, and various veils. However, in today's world of transparency, such tactics no longer work. Customers are well aware of their wants, needs, and expectations, and they're not afraid to call out organizations that fall short. Companies would be better served by willingly examining their own shadows, acknowledging their shortcomings, recognizing the cost of those shortcomings, and honoring the victims of those shadows. It's low-energy behavior to disregard employees' "work-life" balance and fail to live up to company values. We must call out these practices and stop perpetuating them simply because they've always been done this way. It's time for a change because toxicity is no longer sustainable or profitable. One 2023 study showed that American companies lost $1.8 trillion in a single year due to employee turnover.[5]

The cost to companies is immense as employees increasingly prioritize their own values. By fostering fear-based environments where people are afraid to speak up, try new things, or be seen as disruptive, we have stifled creativity and innovation in organizations. Healthier people make better employees, yet we continue to accept burnout as the norm. As someone who has grappled with complex health issues throughout my life, I've had to set boundaries to maintain my well-being. My doctor even refers to me as the healthiest sick person he's ever known. In corporate spaces, I've always made sure to take my lunch breaks, block an hour for myself every morning, and avoid meetings after four o'clock. These standards allow me to function at my

---

[5] Bengfort, Holly. "Employee retention: The real cost of losing an employee." PeopleKeep.com, April 2024 https://www.peoplekeep.com/blog/employee-retention-the-real-cost-of-losing-an-employee

highest level, even when working long hours. Overworking, which is often a trauma-informed behavior, is something I lean towards, but the boundaries I set for myself have made me a better worker.

As a manager, I held similar expectations for my employees. I often conducted outdoor or walking meetings, which proved to be extremely productive. My approach was to work with adults who could manage their own lives, and if I needed to micromanage someone, I would likely let them go. Regardless of age or experience, the team members I supported were exceptional because they felt empowered and knew that I cared about them and their lives. They were great employees because they were allowed to manage their health. There are better ways to do things these days, and while some traditional leadership styles might still work in certain environments, they haven't transitioned well to the corporate world.

This book is for leaders and managers who want to create better businesses, people working in Corporate America who want to feel better, and employees who want to feel empowered and become leaders. We need to have hard conversations, even if they're uncomfortable. We must slow down to advance rather than trying to build the bus while driving it. The bus isn't even running anymore; we're merely stagnating. In this context, we need to be open to the possibilities for change and recognize that just because we've always done something a certain way, this doesn't mean there aren't new approaches and ideas worth exploring.

CHAPTER 1

DREAM JOB

"The path from dreams to success does exist. May you have the vision to find it, the courage to get on to it, and the perseverance to follow it."
– Kalpana Chawla, First Indian-born American Woman Astronaut

Doing the Things

Growing up in America, we are presented with a predetermined path to the corporate world. While different people may have various paths, this particular one is pretty clear: go to school, get great grades, work incredibly hard to get into a top college, graduate with honors, and land the "Dream Job." Many people are expected to follow this path, and they are told it is the best way to achieve success. This expectation stems from the belief that this path is secure, embodying the American Dream of growing up, getting a great job, buying a home, starting a family, having a secure life, retiring, and leaving a lovely legacy. This is the promise of "Doing the Things" and following the path.

It's a great dream, but it leaves a lot of truth in the shadows. It ignores that this idealized path to Corporate America is unobtainable for many people. However, even for the unbelievably driven individuals capable of manifesting through discipline and action, the process is still fraught with challenges. While many steps in the process haven't changed, doing everything possible to get into the best college has become increasingly difficult with each successive generation. This process occurs at a time when individuals don't know much about themselves, yet they are making decisions that will shape the rest of their life. Depending on your influences, choosing the best college could mean a lot of different things, but its importance is clear.[6]

Admitting Admissions

Historically, the college admissions process has had its share of challenges and controversy, and many negative perceptions still persist. In June 2023, the Supreme Court, in a widely controversial ruling, effectively outlawed Affirmative Action, which allowed colleges and universities to consider race as a factor in admissions decisions.[7] Gen Z, the generation currently enrolling in college and the youngest generation entering the workforce, has a generally negative view of the admissions process, with a majority believing that it is heavily biased toward the wealthy and the privileged.[8] There are systemic issues with bias and selection from all viewpoints. The perception of bias in the college admissions process, regardless of how it is expressed or why, weakens the integrity of the process.

Perception matters. When considering access, cost, and affordability of colleges, the perception is that attending college has become phenomenally expensive, and the better the college, the more inaccessible it is. Scandals have occurred where the wealthy were able to pay money to get their children into

---

[6] JP. "NACAC College Admission Process Survey." National Association for College Admission Counseling (NACAC), 22 Aug. 2023, www.nacacnet.org/nacac-college-admission-process-survey/.

[7] Howe, Amy. "Supreme Court Strikes Down Affirmative Action Programs in College Admissions." *SCOTUSblog*, 29 June 2023, www.scotusblog.com/2023/06/supreme-court-strikes-down-affirmative-action-programs-in-college-admissions/.

[8] "Most Young People Think College Admissions Decisions Are Biased, Report Finds." *Bestcolleges.com*, www.bestcolleges.com/news/analysis/young-people-think-college-admissions-are-biased/.

the colleges they wanted.[9] It is considered such a significant issue that celebrities and wealthy professionals were willing to lie and go to prison in an attempt to ensure their children went to the "right school." Their actions, taken without apparent fear of consequence, reveal much about their values and integrity. However, schools and society also share culpability in this by ignoring the deeper consequences of this system. Studies show that the overall perception of the value of higher education is declining, and as it does, colleges and universities are having to adjust accordingly.

For example, education is judged in a way that elevates the idea of going to college as better than other types of education, such as trade schools. In many cases, these skills provide stability, even lucrative opportunities, and can be much more accessible and affordable than college. Trade schools and other learning environments where you learn a particular trade, like plumbing or massage therapy, aren't celebrated in our society in the same way we promote the college experience. Even junior or community colleges can feel like a failure to a young person who has been conditioned to believe that getting into a "great college" is the only path. I received my graphic design training through a community college that had an exceptional visual communication and design program. I was dumbfounded to discover that several of my classmates at the community college had bachelor's degrees from our local state university for the same degree in visual communication and art. They were coming to the community college because their bachelor's degrees only taught them theory, not application. They didn't know how to put any of these concepts or ideas into practice and were attending a community college to learn how. Many of them expressed frustration because after they graduated, they couldn't find jobs in their desired field. We also learned theory, but when we graduated, we could quickly get jobs with much less debt.

---

[9] Taylor, Kate. "College Admissions Scandal." *The New York Times*, 8 Oct. 2019, www.nytimes.com/news-event/college-admissions-scandal.

Degrees are valuable and important, but certifications and specializations can be, too, especially in areas like technology, healthcare, and design. Many talented IT engineers may not have four-year college degrees or better, but they are well-certified and make a very good living. This is part of why I believe that "The Doing of the Things," this path that's drilled into us, in fact, eliminates possibilities instead of creating them for individuals and organizations. The "Things" have the capacity to produce an enormous amount of stress because so many people feel compelled to go down this preset path. These days, for the average person or family to follow that path, they have to decide to go into debt by taking on student loans. It seems strange that as a society, we think this is healthy or beneficial. We place an enormous amount of debt on people before they've ever really been taught how to make or manage money. Functionally, there are real costs associated with this. The average amount of federal debt per graduating student is around $37,000, and it's closer to $50,000 for private loans. What's worse is that 20 years after graduation, the average debt is still around $20,000.[10]

A lifelong choice, or at least a 20+ year fiscal commitment, is made without substantial life experience or any guarantees. This is not necessarily a bad thing if you believe in your investment. You might be making this choice about something that you understand and want to do passionately. You may really want to be a marine biologist and go into marine biology study, or be passionate about numbers and business and pursue an MBA or accounting degree. These may be your passion, and that's great. However, many people follow a path because somebody told them it will give them the best chance at earning the most money, the fastest, or the longest. Some people are fulfilling somebody else's unfulfilled dream. Others don't know enough about themselves to know what they want to learn, but the pressure to decide is immense. Some are told the only path to success is to be an engineer or a

---

[10] Hanson, Melanie. "Average Student Loan Debt." *EducationData.org*, 22 May 2023, educationdata.org/average-student-loan-debt#:~:text=The%20average%20federal%20student%20loan.

doctor, even when they know they are creative and expressive. The message many receive is that they must take this path because it is the stable path that's going to give them everything. If they become an artist, they're just going to starve and die poor. There are some realities that bear out this fear-based advice. For example, according to a University of Houston article on students' dream job perceptions, only 2% of the workforce is employed in "the arts," though I would challenge how we are defining creative and artistic work.[11]

Regardless, when a choice is based on that kind of thinking, it is rooted in fear. Choices made from fear are often self-limiting because the value beyond the fear itself cannot be seen. If safety is always paramount, then survival is the only solution. Maybe you do want to be an artist or do creative work, and you believe in yourself enough to know that you're not going to starve. You're talented and creative, and you're going to go down that creative path with or without the support. Maybe you're driven by innovation or things unknown and learn best through experimentation and exploration. These types of self-awareness should be considered. People are driven by many things, and I have known several people who had a strong sense of their identity at a young age. Often, they seem to have in common one of two things: they come from an emotionally healthy family system that allowed them to develop their core identity in a safe and supportive environment, or they had some sort of experience in their life that provided a unique perspective and deeper personal insight. It could be trauma or personal pain that allowed them to see a problem differently, or some other type of transformational experience, but they're driven by that purpose. Occasionally, it is a combination of the two, which is especially powerful.

There are many different situations that put a person in the position to make these choices, but ultimately, it's about obtaining this dream job. This

---

[11] Fickman, Laurie, "The Job You Want vs. the Job You Get." University of Houston, uh.edu/news-events/stories/2021/june-2021/06242021-dream-job-not-reality-kevin-hoff.php.

job is the projection of what you think is the perfect job for *you*. How well you know yourself is going to determine your ability to manifest it. If your dream job is based on your purpose, creativity, or innovation, and it's because you understand something deep about yourself, you are more likely to manifest a job that will become your dream job, regardless of what you end up doing. This isn't judging anyone who dreams of working in Corporate America because there is a lot of purpose happening across organizations in all industries, and I know plenty of people who love their work and the companies they work for. But the system is not currently working as advertised for a lot of people – workers and leaders alike – so it is worth examining, and the best place to begin an examination is within ourselves.

When you don't know yourself or you're making choices based on someone else's experience, or because you feel conditioned to do something a certain way, you are working from an emotional disadvantage. Family system pressure can make it harder because we don't want to disappoint the people we love. You may find yourself struggling, and your idea of a dream job might shift many times. It's possible that you determine that your dream job doesn't exist for you. If you are never able to connect with that aspect of who you are – the self who understands at a higher level what it is that really allows you to thrive – you may get caught up in a repeating cycle of dissatisfaction.

For the most part, our dreams of the future don't really begin with ourselves. The ideas that shape how we idealize our lives are developed at a very early age. When we're pre-verbal, we are taking in information and observations from our family systems and from our community systems. We look at our parents and their experiences and, without knowing, we take on their expectations and values. We also allow our social circles, media, and the larger community to influence how we define success. How we approach our dreams of the future depends on whether we're moving towards a vision with a clear perspective on where we're going.

Sometimes, people are trying to escape a situation, and maybe they know that there's something better out there, but they might not know what it is. Many of our hopes and dreams will be defined by our conscious and unconscious behaviors and actions. From the moment we exist, we start behaving in ways that we believe are going to help us survive. We do this instinctively. We do things that we may or may not be consciously aware of in order to get our needs met and for people to understand who we are. We need to be able to project the right persona in order to get others to respond to us in the ways that we want them to. Another key thing that is often dismissed is the relevance of our actual dreams – the dreams we have at night while we're asleep. They can give us valuable information about ourselves. This is also true of unconscious behavior and the things we do to try to affect our lives, whether we know it or not.

Dream Job Realities

Corporate America has gone through many transitions and will continue to evolve, but during the 1980s, there was a significant shift that impacted how organizations related to their workforce. Up to the 1980s, companies invested in their employees. They saw the value of doing that, and they had a system of accountability. If an employee was willing to commit their best, most productive years of service to an organization, the organization would make sure that individual would be able to retire and live out a comfortable life. This was the value agreement they had, and it was done through defined benefit plans called Pension Plans. These plans were seen as structured and stable, and through them, employees had a clear understanding of what would be there waiting for them at the end of their careers, in retirement.

In the early '80s, businesses started moving away from these types of plans and towards 401(k) Retirement Plans. They did this for practical reasons. Pension plans were very difficult and costly to administer. Depending on the health of the business over time, businesses might not be able to honor the pension plans. There are even tragic examples in history of companies going out of business and their employees losing everything. For reasons of liability and economics, companies started moving away from assuming that responsibility. As 401(k)s became standard, it reduced employees' security because 401(k)s were tied to the market and to market fluctuations. It also caused the employee to assume more responsibility by requiring them to contribute to their own retirement plans.

There are logical reasons why businesses would have made these choices, and there are even plausible reasons why employees might want more responsibility over their retirement planning. But the access and affordability of these programs are very misaligned. Current data shows that only about 10% of workers have access to structured pension plans.[12] A little more than 50% of American workers actually participate in 401(k) retirement plans, but about 50% of American workers don't have access to them or they can't participate because it's expensive, and they may not see that they have the ability to make that contribution.[13]

There are also generational differences and divisions in perspectives on this because these benefits have shifted over time. We've also seen employee values shifting. Different generations experienced different value systems. When we consider pension plans, retirement, and how they are viewed in Corporate America today, the Baby Boomer generation was really the last to commonly have pensions. While not everybody had access to benefits, for that generation, it was pretty common for companies to have pension plans for

[12] White, Martha C. "The Pension: That Rare Retirement Benefit Gets a Fresh Look." *The New York Times*, 24 Nov. 2023, https://www.nytimes.com/2023/11/24/business/pension-retirement.html

[13] The Economics Daily, "73 Percent of Civilian Workers Had Access to Retirement Benefits in 2023." U.S. Bureau of Labor Statistics, 29 Sep. 2023, www.bls.gov/opub/ted/2023/73-percent-of-civilian-workers-had-access-to-retirement-benefits-in-2023.htm.

their employees. Gen X literally witnessed the dissolution of pension plans. Pension plans went away, generally speaking, during my teen years.

I came into the workforce in the late '80s and early '90s. By the time I did so, pension plans were already considered rare or non-existent. Millennials, Gen Y, and now Gen Z have never known the existence of this type of security. It's just never been a part of their lives. That generational divide and perspective makes it very difficult for each generation to relate to what the other generation is experiencing in this context.

For many people, the system feels completely upside-down. I think there are companies working to try to solve this problem, but we still have unbalanced compensation issues and an aging population that is unprepared for the realities of retirement.[14] We have a workforce that is under extreme pressure, where more than 80% of working Americans report suffering from workplace stress.[15] Another challenge is that these days, the median job tenure is around four years. So, assuming you took out a student loan, in 20 years on average, you're going to have to work at least five jobs to pay off only half of that debt. In that sense, it's a twisted system. It doesn't really work anymore. It's not supporting business and it's not supporting the workforce. Our dream jobs are becoming nightmares.

---

[14] Haltzel, L. "As the Population Ages, More Workers Are Unprepared for Retirement. Can States Help Close That Gap?" The Century Foundation, 25 Oct. 2023, tcf.org/content/report/as-the-population-ages-more-workers-are-unprepared-for-retirement-can-states-help-close-that-gap/#:~:text=are%20being%20used.-.

[15] Boyd, Danielle. "Workplace Stress." The American Institute of Stress, 2022, www.stress.org/workplace-stress#:~:text=83%25%20of%20US%20workers%20suffer.

Action Items and Journal Prompts: Chapter 1

Reflections

- Describe your family culture related to working. What were you taught was important?

- Did you have a job that you dreamed about when you were a kid? Did it change? Why or why not?

- If you could choose, would you be doing something else for work? If so, write about what this would be. If not, list the ways your current job is serving your needs.

- Are you willing to take a risk with your career? What is the riskiest career decision you have made? How did it work out for you?

- What does retirement look like to you? Describe your vision. Is your vision different from what you've been taught or seen other people experience? In what ways?

Actions

- **Investigate Your Dream.** If you have a dream job you're not doing, find someone who is already doing it. Reach out to them and ask them to share their thoughts and feelings about their job. Is it their dream job, too?

- **Start With Intention.** Begin a simple gratitude and manifestation practice. Keep it simple. Consistency has more value than complexity.

CHAPTER 2

PERFECT CANDIDATE

"Leaders should strive for authenticity over perfection."
– Sheryl Sandberg, Author and former COO of Meta Platforms

If you're going to land the dream job, you better become the perfect candidate. Or at least, that's what we're told.

When I think about my own career identity and how it has evolved over the years, I'm not sure I had any idea of who I was in the corporate space until I had worked there for quite a while. It felt like I was trying on roles, and in many ways, I was. I believe there are many people who can relate to this and also to the feeling that everyone else has it all figured out. There were pivotal moments early in my career when someone gave me feedback about where I needed to grow or, even more importantly, where I had shown growth, but it was up to me to believe in myself. For a lot of reasons, that wasn't always easy.

I don't think my experience is particularly unique, but, like many of you, it has its own flavor. One thing is true for all of us: we start off as baby humans equipped with egos to help us survive. From this, we begin to subconsciously build and craft personas that express how we can best get our needs met. The crafting and building begin early in our lives – right from the start. We're observing, we're learning, and we're developing the mechanisms and actions that are going to work best to help us advance. We might be taught that we need to be the good girl or the tough boy. We are told that we need to be outspoken, creative, helpful, or quiet. We then take what we're taught and see if it works for us. If it gets our needs met, we lean into that behavior. If it doesn't, we're likely to push it away. We start crafting these personas, and we don't even realize we're doing it. This isn't something that's contrived. Our ego is involved because our ego is always involved in helping us survive.

For many of us, our personas work well until we develop more awareness. For example, our persona helps people know how to relate to us when we show up in social situations. You might be the funny guy, the super-smart girl, the eccentric. These all seem like stereotypes because that is how many people will perceive us, but we are projecting these ideals of who we are. We teach people who we are and how to treat us. Our personas help people understand things about us and, sometimes, make assumptions. This can be frustrating when the assumptions don't feel aligned with who we think we are, which is why stereotypes can be harmful. We may even project different personas for different environments, such as a "Family" persona and a "Friends" persona. There's a lot of compartmentalization occurring, and it's all about survival and needs. As we prepare ourselves to move onto that fast track into the corporate world, we start thinking about how we're going to show up as a professional.

I think, for most people, your first "Corporate" persona is an amalgamation of everything you think is right. It's an infusion of your personality, built on a foundation of what's been modeled in your family system and then accessorized by what you've absorbed through media, social or otherwise. There are many external influences, and you want to present yourself as the ideal candidate: the right look, perfect clothes, a resume or CV that's beyond reproach, and engaging, stimulating profiles. Somewhere in this process, more compartmentalization occurs. We look at ourselves compared to the world around us and begin judging pieces and parts. You think, *This aspect of myself might be too weird, so I better hide it,* or *Everyone seems happy when I do this, so I'll do it even more.* You're told you can't show up and be too emotional, so to compensate, you become stoic instead. This is all happening subconsciously as your ego works to adapt your persona toward the best possible outcome.

You might even try on some roles, like I did. For me, trying on roles is a process of growing and discovering more aspects of who I am. There is no age limit for this practice; it is an ongoing part of your personal evolution. I have seen people redefine themselves at multiple points throughout their careers and lives. For example, it took me some time to find and trust my voice and to understand how I wanted to be seen and heard – how I wanted to show up. It took experience and awareness to learn that about myself, which didn't happen right away.

Something that catches people off guard during any self-examination is their relationships. As you're building your corporate persona, you become more aware of who you know, who knows you, and how they know you. You're transitioning into this new space, and you feel an urgent need to fit into the culture. It's important to you that you're accepted for personal and practical reasons. Sometimes, the people in your life can support that transition, and sometimes they can be an impediment.

Any period in your life when you have to evaluate relationships is layered and emotional, and many of us struggle here. It's important to look at the energy of the people in your life and determine how they support you as you grow and develop into these new roles and expand your persona, especially energetically. Do they lift you up or express constant doubt? As you expand, there will be people who resist your change, preferring that you remain exactly the same, even when that doesn't work for you anymore. Your change means change for them, too. Healthy relationships can adapt to change, and all relationships have a natural course and rhythm. The struggle is with our identity attachment to these relationships that we don't want to relinquish. The process of determining who you are as the perfect candidate also becomes an examination of who you are in your personal relationships. People don't always grow at the same pace, and we aren't all meant to walk the same paths. We bring people into our lives to teach us more about ourselves. Some of those relationships are eternal and are meant to be that way. Some are intended to be transitional. The more you understand the transactional energy of your relationships, the easier it is to identify when they're supporting your health and highest needs and when they're not.

Job Quest

In the midst of all this new information, self-awareness, and personal growth, you also have to define yourself in a very tangible way through resumes and profiles. You're figuring out who you are and what your persona is, but then you have to document it with clarity and know how to pitch yourself and the value you bring. Developing this clarity is challenging. You have to know yourself well, but even more importantly, you have to know who you're presenting yourself to. So, clarity for whom?

These days, people typically find jobs in one of two ways: through networking and referrals or keywords and algorithms. One is highly personal, and the other feels barely human. Each has a strategic approach that works best for it. It's very frustrating for many people to have to craft their profiles and think about themselves in terms of keywords and algorithms. On some level, digital job searches strip humanity out of the job search process. Or at least it can feel that way.

Conversely, having connections and knowing people who can help you isn't necessarily any easier. You might be the perfect candidate, but you won't ever get noticed if you don't have an effective resume or a well-crafted profile. If you don't know the right people, even worse. Job candidates in the workforce these days have to figure out how to balance that and be seen. And then there's the recruiting process.

A third way people find jobs is by being recruited, but that is also highly dependent on a recruiter being able to find you in the first place. I think recruiting is a challenging process and depends on the environment and the type of recruiting that's happening. You may not want to be recruited. I think there's a mythology around being recruited where you feel noticed and wanted. One sees many fairs and career days where they send the recruiters out, and everybody shows up with their resumes. Those people are often trying to bring in a pool of talent. Then there's more targeted recruiting, where the recruiter is looking for a specific candidate. It seems like there's an aspect of recruiting that has a fraternity or sorority "rush" feel to it. These days it may be much more nuanced, but overall, the process is transactional and feels disconnecting in many ways. It's a process that isn't always aligned at a value level with what the employee needs and what the organization needs.

Often, recruiting and talent are a part of human resources. They manage and control that aspect of the business. You may actually be recruited by a human resources person who has been given a job description by a hiring manager. They may not have an in-depth understanding of subtle aspects of the position, but ideally, they are able to assess the values and culture fit between the company and candidate. Occasionally, you're recruited by a hiring manager who is the actual person you will report to. They often know exactly who they need and what they're looking for but may be less focused on larger organizational needs, parameters, or goals. In my experience, in situations where a hiring manager has recruited me, it typically feels more transparent as it relates to both my understanding of the position and the culture.

Recruiting is as much of an art as it is a science, but having clearly stated and aligned values makes the process exponentially more productive for everyone involved. If the values of the culture aren't aligned with the individual, then ultimately, you're going to create turnover because those individuals aren't going to stay very long. A recent study by Leadership IQ showed an important contradiction pertaining to company culture.[16] On the one hand, the study showed that more than 50% of companies' employees say that innovation is a core company value. On the other hand, a large percentage of managers interviewed said that they fear hiring innovative people. They indicated that innovative people ask too many questions and aren't going to just put their heads down and get the job done.

For the average manager, innovative people are going to be too disruptive. This is an example of a real value misalignment. If you have an organization that espouses innovation but doesn't want to bring on innovators, you're going to end up with big problems. If they do bring on innovators, those innovators are not going to be valued or appreciated properly because the company really isn't in alignment with its own value system. Companies have to take a step back and understand how that creates incongruences in a way that ultimately turns into toxicity over time. Hiring is often reactive for short-term needs. If companies were more proactive about recruiting and taking more time with it, they would obtain better results. When companies really take the time to align their value systems with the employees that they're trying to recruit, they have less turnover, and the overall health of the organization is better. What's more, these days, the script has really been flipped in the recruiting and hiring process. Workers are reviewing companies with just as much discernment, if not more, than companies have been reviewing workers. When we talk about slowing down to advance, COVID was a very interesting period for us, and it allowed people to take a pause and evaluate aspects of their lives. They could experience a genuine "work-life" balance. In that pause, individuals began to evaluate their own value systems, where those value systems were being challenged, and where they were being supported. We've seen all sorts of headlines over the

---

[16] "Managers Don't Love Innovators." *Leadership IQ*,
www.leadershipiq.com/blogs/leadershipiq/managers-don-t-love-innovators.

last few years about quiet quitting, the Great Resignation, and people refusing to do burnout-level work anymore.

I saw a meme recently where someone who was told that they were *not allowed* to work from home, even though their job could be done remotely, simply stopped doing all after-hours work from home. When their boss questioned them about not responding to an after-hours email, they responded that they were NOT ALLOWED to work from home, showing these arbitrary rules can sometimes cut both ways. People are starting to set some boundaries around their time, energy, and workspaces. Gen Z is now in the workforce, and they are really shaking things up. Many people still probably think that millennials are 25 years old, but millennials are actually in their 40s. Gen Z is the newest generation to enter the workforce.

Research has found that 87% of Gen Z workers will leave a job if it does not align with their values. That's a stunning shift, especially if we look at previous generations. I saw a reel recently on Instagram or TikTok, and it made me laugh out loud. It was comparing Gen X, Millennial, and Gen Z employees and how they showed up to work based on timing. The start time of the day was 7 a.m., and it showed Gen X running into the office totally stressed out. You can tell that they've already been stressed out for hours before they even made it to work, and it's only six in the morning. They're an hour early, they're running into the office, and they're going to get right to their day.

Then we see a Millennial showing up. They're super casual, you know, they've got their coffee, and they're all chill. They're glancing at their watch. It's exactly 6:59 a.m. They're walking in the door at 7 a.m., right on time, ready to start their day.

Then Gen Z shows up, maybe two or three hours later. They don't know what time it is, and they don't really care; they're going to walk in and get their job done, too. They're just going to do it in a different way, perhaps with a lot less stress. Their values seem more aligned in that sense. It made me laugh, and I related to it quite a bit. As a Gen Xer, I was definitely conditioned to be a Good Corporate Citizen, and good corporate citizens show up early.

Another part of this process of being the perfect candidate and trying to find this perfect job is that there's a big divide right now between the digital world and the personal space. On a personal level, there's a lot that you can do to position yourself as a perfect candidate, just based on who you know. There's a lot of perceived bias in hiring practices, and companies have tried to bring in DEI initiatives and various other programs to mitigate that bias. However, when an issue requires forced intervention, it indicates that the underlying problem still persists. The bias remains present, and the problem will only be truly solved when the bias is no longer an issue, which is not yet the case. Building your network is going back to knowing who to know. It is important to build a network and to find value-matched peers and mentors who will honor your relationship authentically. Meaningful connections and thoughtful relationships are the ones that hold the most opportunity for your growth. When you're present for people, people become more present for you. It's important to attend and participate in your community, including your business community. For example, are there business organizations that support the industry that you're in, or does your industry support different causes where you can be a participant? It's not just about landing the best job but also about truly showing up as an individual and becoming part of that community.

On the digital side, things have become challenging because digital job descriptions are mostly just based on algorithms. As individuals, I think that we resist being cataloged like that. Nobody wants to be perceived as an algorithmic output or a set of keywords. It's another area where Corporate America is going to have to figure out how to adapt and make it better because a lot of great talent gets overlooked because of bad resumes. Unless you're hiring a resume writer, this feels like an extremely arbitrary way to overlook talented people. AI is going to be very interesting in this space because AI may be able to bridge a little bit of that gap. While on the surface it seems like it's moving further away from that human connection, AI can be trained in a way to do vetting and assessing that goes beyond simple keywords and algorithms while also eliminating bias. This is already happening and it will effectively change the recruiting landscape.

So, as job seekers, once we have figured out all of that chaos, created our perfect persona, and gotten the profiles and the resumes in place. We've fed all the algorithms, we've met with the recruiters, we've talked to the hiring managers, we've gone through our day of interviews with people that we'll probably never see again, and we finally got the job.

I think, for most people, the day you get that job offer is really an exciting moment, even if it's not your dream job. There's so much work, energy, and effort that goes into your presentation and process. That first day of work, we go in very optimistic. Many people go in with their best foot forward with this ideal. Everything is new, and there are real possibilities. Those first impressions early on are critical to how you either succeed and thrive in that space or whether it becomes diminishing. Company culture first impressions are interesting because, just like people, companies often try to put on their best, shiny face. They really want to put their best self forward. When we go through the recruiting process, a lot of what we're told is, "This is how great our culture is, and these are what our values are." This is how organizations represent themselves. There may be messaging around purpose, and all of that is very enticing and captivating. When we go into that organization, we're looking at that company through those lenses, and we want to see the validation of that messaging. I think it's very important that you stay in observation mode for a while when you start in a new company. Let yourself absorb the culture and also pay attention to how you show up in that culture, to the energy that you bring with you to the environment that you're in. This is vital.

Action Items and Journal Prompts: Chapter 2

Reflections

- How do you define perfect? What were you taught about perfection in your family system?

- What aspects of yourself do you try to hide from others? What are you protecting yourself from by doing this?

- What are three keywords that you would use to describe yourself that you would never put on your resume? How are you judging these words?

- What do you find more challenging, giving feedback or receiving it? Why?

- If you are someone who hires people, how does the idea of finding "the perfect person for the job" influence or impede your hiring process?

Actions

- **Update** Ritually. Set a reminder to update your resume every six months from now on, regardless of your goals or employment status. Maintain a record of your achievements. If you have one, review and update your LinkedIn profile every six months, as well.

- "Improv" Yourself. Sign up for a local or online Improv class. It will be one of the most valuable skills and experiences you give yourself - personally or professionally.

CHAPTER 3

THE MISFITS

"In a crowded marketplace, fitting in is a failure. In a busy marketplace, not standing out is the same as being invisible."
– Seth Godin, American Entrepreneur and Author

We can't talk about the perfect corporate candidate without talking a little bit about some of the non-traditional candidates who find themselves in the corporate world. These people are highly valuable to the corporate world, but there are not always easy entry points or welcoming spaces for them. In many ways, they are the misfits of corporate culture, but they have something unique to offer. Here are a few examples and profiles of non-traditional corporate employees:

Entrepreneurs

To begin with, many "Entrepreneurs" never work in the corporate world; they start as and remain "Entrepreneurs." People start businesses, create innovative products, and believe in themselves enough to always step into this space. However, there are many people who aspire to be "Entrepreneurs" but instead follow a traditional path into the corporate world. This may be due to conditioning, fear, or a genuine belief that it is the right path for them. So, they Do all the Things: they go to college, earn the degree, make the plan, and then enter the corporate space, where they have a realization. They see how everything works – the processes, functions, and operations – and realize they have their own vision and believe they can do it better. "Entrepreneurs" would rather be their own bosses and control their energy and outcomes. Many do not stay long in corporate environments because they are not challenged or satisfied in that space. They may feel frustrated because they do not fit into the corporate culture, which is usually risk averse. If the "Entrepreneur" is in a toxic culture, exposure to career-limiting behaviors and micromanagement will be intolerable to their nature.

When "Entrepreneurs" stay in the corporate space, it's often because they feel nurtured and valued and are given opportunities to express their entrepreneurial nature. They become the "Corporate Innovator" persona because they are visionary by nature and will identify opportunities and solve problems before they occur. They're willing to take calculated risks and tend to be highly self-motivated. "Entrepreneurs" don't need a lot of management because they get things done. It's not uncommon for "Entrepreneurs" to stay in the corporate world, become innovators, and then get promoted to leadership roles.

One thing that business leaders should consider is the value of having innovative people in their organizations. As noted above, a recent study showed that while a majority of people indicated that innovation is a "significant" value to their organization, data overwhelmingly showed that leaders and managers don't actually want innovative risk-takers as employees.[17] It's something of a contradiction or what I would call a deep misalignment of values. It seems disingenuous to promote a value that would attract a certain type of person and then not support or activate that value. Companies that truly want to attract and retain innovative employees need to

---

[17] "Managers Don't Love Innovators." *Leadership IQ*,
www.leadershipiq.com/blogs/leadershipiq/managers-don-t-love-innovators.

consider their culture and whether it is designed to support this type of person
– and companies that don't need to do so, too. Saying you value innovation
while not supporting it is either delusional or dishonest and will create issues.

Developers and Coders

This talented group of individuals fits the non-traditional candidate
definition because they're a little bit of an offshoot of the "Entrepreneur," even
though they differ in certain ways. While most developers have at least a
bachelor's degree, many begin learning to code in early education and thus
enter higher education with these skills already developed. Others are self-
trained or self-taught, having been certified through self-paced courses or in
certified training programs. This group is disciplined about learning their
craft and exhibits the ability to be independent and flexible in their work.
Approximately 70% of developers and coders are employed full-time within
corporations, but according to a recent survey, the number of independent
developers is on the rise.[18]

With hybrid working environments becoming both necessary and
controversial, developers are finding they have more flexibility in managing
their output. They may not possess the entrepreneurial spirit in the same way
entrepreneurs do, but they offer a high-value service that allows them to
maintain independence in their training and skill set. Developers have the
ability to be fluid in their interactions with the corporate world and, in some
ways, how they enter the corporate environment. I believe they don't need to
follow the traditional track, and the trend moving forward will likely favor
their empowerment. Companies that wish to retain this group of talented
individuals will need to recognize the importance they place on flexibility and

---

[18] "Stack Overflow Developer Survey 2023." *Stack Overflow*, 2023, survey.stackoverflow.co/2023/.

training, and be willing to make those changes or investments to better align with their values and needs.

Creatives and Artists

Of all of the groups who may identify most as feeling like misfits, creatives and artists tend to express this sentiment the most. The corporate world desperately needs creativity, yet traditionally, it has not provided a nurturing environment for individuals with a creative mindset. Creatives have often been misunderstood by corporate culture, whether you're talking about the over-generalized "marketing people" or, more specifically, graphic designers, web designers, content writers, meeting and event planners, product designers, or any other role that demands intuitive skills, creative instincts, and design-based thinking. Although these roles balance highly technical skills with deep creative and conceptual work, creative individuals in non-creative corporate spaces are frequently undervalued and underutilized. For instance, executives' all-too-common marketing request is to "make something look pretty." It's so common that it's a cliché, but it's also true in a very particular way that illustrates that people don't always understand the full value and impact of deep creativity, as well as how innovation and strategic thinking drive it.

Currently, many believe that creativity in the corporate world faces potential threats, especially with considerations around AI and its role. Concerns abound, fueled by articles and headlines about AI job takeovers and risks to copyright and intellectual property rights. According to a Goldman Sachs report, 26% of repetitive tasks related to creative jobs could be replaced by Generative AI.[19] However, the report also noted that, as with previous

[19] Goldman Sachs. *The Recent Emergence of Generative Artificial Intelligence (AI) Raises Whether We.* 26 Mar. 2023. https://www.goldmansachs.com/intelligence/topics/artificial-intelligence.html#:~:text=Generative%20artificial%20intelligence%20has%20the,in%20the%20years%20that%20follow.

technological shifts, the elimination of some jobs would lead to the creation of new, different roles. Forward-thinking creatives are adopting AI as a tool, just as they would any other, learning how to enhance their creative talents with it. A comment overheard at a CX/EX conference summed it up: "AI won't replace people; people who know how to use AI will replace those who don't." This perspective seems more accurate than the dire "AI is taking over." Still, when we look at how corporations value creative people, there's this struggle of placing the right amount of value and understanding how to measure that value. The introduction of AI calls this into question even more. Can human creativity simply be replaced with augmented intelligence, and if so, what are the real costs of such a replacement?

One issue with corporate cultures not valuing creative individuals is the lack of inclusive planning. The emphasis on intellectual and strategic thinking often limits projects that rely on creative output. When organizations plan in isolation or in silos, they restrict the insights and impacts available from some of their most innovative members. In the last decade, as marketing and technology have increasingly overlapped and required collaboration, these perceptions have started to change, with creative roles being recognized as strategic rather than merely tactical. There's a growing understanding of the creative psyche and the space needed for true innovation and problem-solving. Creative individuals can navigate the corporate world with or without business degrees, but a grasp of business practices is critical to their success in this space. However, they can be self-taught and demonstrate their skills and talents in ways that degrees don't always represent.

Organizations that impose unreasonable demands on their creative staff due to poor planning that results in unnecessary stress will face greater challenges in recruiting and retaining individuals for these roles. Many people who identify as creative also see themselves as highly sensitive individuals, and this combination can be detrimental to a toxic corporate culture with lasting effects. Companies that claim to value creativity must consider where to invest their time, energy, or financial resources to support it. Understanding and respecting the needs of creative individuals will help organizations foster a culture of respect for creative contributions.

Non-degreed People

A big talent group that gets overlooked in Corporate America is people without formal degrees. I see this as self-limiting for individuals and for organizations. I value education and hold great respect for the achievement of obtaining a degree, and I also recognize that a degree is an essential requirement for certain roles, a point I would never dispute. Jobs such as physicians, lawyers, architects, and other professions requiring extensive education, intensive study, internships, and ongoing learning are undoubtedly critical. When hiring, I certainly consider education as part of evaluating whether a candidate is suitable for a position, and I view it as a fair criterion. However, it becomes self-limiting when organizations insist on educational qualifications in ways that exclude experienced, talented individuals who are well-suited for roles yet lack a formal degree.

The prevalence of bots, keywords, and digital recruiting exacerbates this issue. If the requisite education is missing from your resume or LinkedIn profile, you're likely to be overlooked automatically. Currently, about 78% of companies still require candidates to have a bachelor's degree, but there are clear indications that this trend is changing.[20] More organizations are eliminating degree requirements in favor of a skills-based hiring approach, which values overall experience and skills alongside education. As talent pools evolve, more companies will seek to tap into traditionally underutilized talent markets. Until such changes become widespread, networking and personal referrals can help overcome that barrier. This is where knowing who you

[20] Harmon, A. "Why Multiple Companies Aren't Requiring College Degrees Anymore." *Recruiter.com*, www.recruiter.com/recruiting/why-multiple-companies-arent-requiring-college-degrees-anymore/.

know can make a significant difference. Many individuals without degrees secure opportunities within organizations through effective networking and meaningful connections.

If companies struggle to attract talent, it's time to reevaluate the self-limiting practices that are keeping the best talent away from you. How are you accommodating the needs of your employees? Are you ignoring opportunities based on staid and dated beliefs?

For individuals without degrees, it's crucial to recognize your value and confront your self-limiting beliefs. Present yourself fearlessly in ways that can't be ignored. Learn how to promote yourself with confidence and be unapologetic about the experience that put you where you are today. It has immense value – sometimes more value than a degree can provide. Don't let other people define you. Know yourself and believe.

Influencers and Counterculture

There are two more groups I want to discuss that I believe are often misunderstood by corporate culture: influencers and counterculture individuals. These groups are relevant because they are vexing to Corporate America, which is always trying to figure out how to capitalize on them, control them, and, in the case of Influencers, how to create them. They see the magnitude of connection that they have with their communities. Influencers are out there developing their own brands and putting their identities on display. The real savvy influencers are initiating trends or staying ahead of them. I think we'll continue to see that merger of relationships with influencers and corporations because there's such an appeal.

As we seek more authenticity and connection with people, influencers fill an emotional void. I think that's where they grab the heart and soul of their audience. They're putting themselves out there, speaking to people, and connecting with them in ways that feel relatable and personal. They do this in a more authentic way than brands have traditionally tried to speak to their audience, and it resonates in a very different way. It will be interesting to see if corporations are able to figure that out or if – like usual – they just end up diluting their power by over-consumption.

Just this week, I saw how corporations like General Mills are working with influencers to promote the "anti-diet" trend, and it's having a significant impact.[21] With a focus on food-shaming and hashtags like #NoBadFoods, analysis shows a measured increase in nutritionists promoting these concepts, along with products, describing them as mostly paid. For me, these scenarios boil down to truth and authenticity in terms of sustainability. I think influencers add value in our society, especially as they can influence and educate with such powerful reach. As we see more alignment between corporations and influencers, it's important that the value alignments are more than transactional. Influencers need to be truly invested in what they promote to maintain truth with their followers.

Counter to Corporate Culture

When referring to "counterculture," specifically in business spaces, I am speaking about individuals who have been unfairly judged by mainstream Corporate culture. Often, these groups establish their own cultures as a defense against irrational judgments, leading them to feel alienated from corporate culture and to mistrust it. However, it's interesting how corporate culture has been slowly shifting over time. Many individuals historically marginalized in the corporate world are now claiming their power and making their presence felt in spaces like the boardroom and the C-suite. Arbitrary standards rooted in bigotry and racism, such as policies on

---

[21] "As Obesity Rises, Big Food and Dietitians Push "Anti-Diet" Advice." *Washington Post*, 3 Apr. 2024, www.washingtonpost.com/wellness/2024/04/03/diet-culture-nutrition-influencers-general-mills-processed-food/.

hairstyles and other forms of personal cultural expression, have been challenged. Despite some progress, much work remains.

For example, a study published in the *Harvard Business Review* found that black women's hairstyles were "two and a half times more likely to be perceived as unprofessional."[22] Even worse, the study noted that one-fifth of their survey participants had been sent home due to having "unprofessional" hair. It is important to clarify that I am not suggesting the black community is a "counterculture" in the traditional definition of the word. The black community encompasses a race of distinct cultures with diverse individuals. Labeling black hairstyles as "counter" to corporate culture is a cultural expression of racism within business. This issue is compounded by the corporate response to groups that genuinely represent countercultures, highlighting the need for a deeper understanding and acceptance within corporate environments.[23]

For example, tattoos, once primarily associated with service members and biker gangs in Western culture, are now seen as symbols of counterculture, and have also become increasingly common in corporate environments. This trend is likely to only increase, with nearly 40% of individuals aged 18–34 already sporting tattoos.[24] Whereas tattoos were once an immediate deterrent and were required to be hidden, if allowed at all, they have now become so mainstream that the majority of employers have eliminated restrictions on tattoos completely, as long as they are not deemed offensive. This represents a significant cultural shift within a generation, indicating that employers are recognizing that personal expression of who

---

[22] Asare, Janice Gassam. "How Hair Discrimination Affects Black Women at Work." *Harvard Business Review*, 10 May 2023, hbr.org/2023/05/how-hair-discrimination-affects-black-women-at-work.

[23] "Definition of Counterculture | Dictionary.com." *Dictionary.com*, 2019, www.dictionary.com/browse/counterculture.

[24] "Tattoos in the Workplace Statistics in 2022." *TeamStage*, 13 Apr. 2022, teamstage.io/tattoos-in-the-workplace-statistics/.

you are – even in ways that might not fit into the "suit and tie" tradition of corporate culture – does not necessarily dictate your talent or value or worth in an organization. However, tattoos represent a choice in personal expression, unlike natural hairstyles. Today, only 4% of people with tattoos report experiencing discrimination, compared to one-fifth of black women who are sent home for their hairstyles, highlighting a clear problem. Such disparities are unacceptable and contribute to how we judge each other and ourselves within this culture, creating costly toxicity. However, we have the choice to see and act on the enormous opportunities this awareness offers for growth in Corporate America and beyond.

By its truest definition, counterculture individuals are often innovative and highly creative thinkers who may increasingly distance themselves from corporate culture, possibly more than the corporate world excludes them. The same article on tattoos in the corporate sector mentioned the "cool factor" of having tattooed employees, suggesting it makes some brands appear more authentic. This notion made me roll my eyes. It would be amusing if it weren't indicative of a larger issue. There has been a slight shift, but corporate culture still has a long way to go in truly understanding and embracing what it even means to be counterculture.

We Are All Ego Here

I want to discuss ego and business, but I can't do so without addressing how our egos affect us personally, and how they relate to our identity and psyche.

As I mentioned, we all have an ego, which plays a crucial role in our survival. Our egos begin developing at a very early age, as soon as we start gaining consciousness. From the moment that we're born, we begin developing our egos to help us meet our needs. The ego acts as a vigilant watchman, constantly monitoring for behavior patterns and energetic connections that either fulfill or fail to meet our needs. As infants, these needs include being fed, nurtured, held, and feeling secure and cared for. Over time, if some of these needs are not met, we may adopt certain behavior patterns, leading our ego to continue acting out these patterns. This process can be subtle and doesn't necessarily stem from big T trauma. However, if our needs remain unmet – due to, for example, the absence of a parent or lack of nurturing – the resulting behavior patterns can become counterproductive and work against us.

Both overactive and underactive egos typically signal unresolved trauma. An out-of-control or completely suppressed ego suggests that it is dominating all aspects of your life, making everything feel chaotic. This condition often stems from unresolved trauma, and you're just acting out. Without addressing the underlying emotions, you will remain in survival mode, governed by unconscious defense mechanisms that maintain detrimental behavior patterns. This leads to emotional reactivity, damaging both personal and professional relationships. Ideally, we want our ego to feel nurtured, safe, and secure. When our ego feels safe, then our higher self can be in control, and we can thrive. Otherwise, we live in a state of anxiety, panic, or distress.

Ego Fairy Tales

With that in mind, let's discuss the role of ego in business. I refer to it as the "ego fairy tales" because the ego is often greatly misunderstood and, in many ways, abused within the business context. We have created these mythologies where egos are either excessively glorified or harshly demonized, and we give them a lot of power. We've all encountered various ego personas: the stereotypical loud, obnoxious individual who is oblivious to others; the fragile, highly emotionally reactive egos, unable to accept criticism; the damaged egos, unpredictable and often described as narcissistic. It's not uncommon for such individuals to act out in abusive ways, seeking to undermine others. These diverse personas are nurtured in odd ways in the corporate world. Some of the greatest and most notorious egos of our time have been memorialized in films and iconographically held up as representations of what it means to be corporate.

When reflecting on prominent egos, Steve Jobs instantly comes to mind. He was an exceptional inventor and a true visionary, founding one of the most influential companies of our time. His innovations have touched nearly everyone in some way, significantly impacting our culture. Yet, Jobs was also known for his notorious ego, which at times proved damaging and disruptive. In 1984, Apple's board decided to diminish his role due to his erratic behavior.[25] He couldn't accept the demotion, so he chose to quit instead and went on to try to start another company. Eventually, he went back to Apple and took them to even greater heights. He had a very turbulent leadership experience, but it is clear that he grew and developed as a leader. He passed too young from pancreatic cancer. To me, it was a great loss because I think we still had so much to learn from him. He had awareness and growth as a leader, moving through deep resistance. In the process of his life transition, he shared some of that wisdom during a commencement speech at Stanford University in 2005. I interpret the following quote as speaking about ego and higher self-awareness.

> *"Remembering that I'll be dead soon is the most important tool I've ever encountered to help me make the big choices in life. Because almost everything – all external expectations, all pride, all fear of embarrassment or failure – these things just fall away in the face of death, leaving only what is truly important. Remembering that you are going to die is the best way I know to avoid the trap of thinking you have something to lose. You are already naked. There is no reason not to follow your heart."*[26] – Steve Jobs

[25] Bajarin, Tim. "Steve Jobs' Firing from Apple vs. Sam Altman's Firing from OpenAI." *Forbes*, 20 Nov. 2023, www.forbes.com/sites/timbajarin/2023/11/20/steve-jobs-firing-from-apple-vs-sam-altmans-firing-from-openai/?sh=4e04f621fa99.

[26] Jobs, Steve. *Stanford University 2005 Commencement Speech*. Stanford University Graduation. Oral.

Whenever I reflect on how egos have been glorified in the worst ways, *The Wolf of Wall Street* immediately comes to mind, a movie based on a true story. I had to do some personal shadow work on how much this film triggered me. It deeply unsettled me. While I recognize and appreciate the narrative as someone's real-life experience, and on one level, I can accept it without judgment, in a deeper way the film profoundly disturbed me. Watching it, I was preoccupied with the consequences of the characters' severely damaged egos: these entirely unaccountable individuals who were not just abusive but celebrated for it. Leonardo DiCaprio's portrayal of vulgarity and immorality as the pinnacle of success in our corporate environment was exceptional. Although the film aims to convey a message of truth-telling and redemption, it seemed to place undue emphasis on rewarding reprehensible behavior. It was a difficult story for me to integrate because I felt value-conflicted watching it. It didn't seem right that this felt more like a celebration of bad behavior than a condemnation. It's one of those weird films that I can objectively call a good movie, while still not feeling good about it and having no desire to see again. That said, I think it has something very relevant to say about Corporate America's unhealthy relationship with the ego.

Higher Self-Perspective

The way that we manage the ego and the way that we truly step into authenticity is by engaging with our higher self. We approach our world through a persona that we project. Our personas are built by our ego. They express our identity, and we put ourselves out there in the way that we think is going to be received best. In doing that, we push away a lot of aspects of our personality that we're taught are bad or that we believe are not going to be useful to us. In some cases, that really works against us, and we end up not using or accessing the best parts of who we are.

An example of that might be that you're taught that creativity doesn't have any value; only logic does. In response, you push creativity aside, and you tell yourself that you're not a creative person at all. Another example is being told that you are good when you are quiet, so you learn to never raise your voice or speak up. This is how your ego is protecting you and keeping you safe from rejection. Your higher self, in contrast, understands that you are a whole being. Your higher self acknowledges and honors the ego, but it also honors your conscious and unconscious mind, your deeper soul, and your spiritual needs. This is not a religious concept, but rather an energetic and agnostic one. Your higher self honors your purpose and it allows you to have a voice. When you are working from your higher self, you are fully present and able to access and express whatever energy you need to. Your higher self maintains safety for the ego in order for you to be able to express yourself in truly authentic ways. We can uncover new insights about ourselves and our personas by observing from the perspective of the higher self. Doing so objectively, we see that we're often repeatedly emotionally activated by other types of personas.

For example, perhaps you're triggered by extremely authoritative people. You know that whenever you're around somebody who just barks out orders, you shut down and become diminutive and quiet. If you realize not everyone responds that way to that individual, you gain more insight about yourself. It may seem obvious why you might act a certain way, but then why doesn't everyone? The more you can understand why you are reacting the way you do, the more ability you have to turn that reaction into an intentional response. Each one of us is having our own individual persona experience, and we're projecting and/or receiving that energy from the people around us. This constant reactive exchange of energy is what allows us to be emotionally triggered, and it's what creates these unconscious behavior patterns.

The concepts of personas and archetypes were developed and popularized by psychologist Carl Jung in the early 1900s. Breaking away from the prevalent Freudian theory of his time, Jung introduced innovative ideas about the psyche, formally presenting the concepts of archetypes and the unconscious mind in 1919.[27] Jung described archetypes as "patterns of instinctual behavior" and considered them universal to all human experience. For example, we can talk about the hero archetype, the lover archetype or the parent archetype. These are all archetypes that everybody experiences. There are thousands of them. There are many, many different types of archetype energy. When I look at corporate archetype energy, I believe that we all put on a persona type that we think is going to work for us.

In the corporate space, we often adopt specific persona types we believe will serve us well. For instance, one might take on the role of the "Office Parent," the "Big Boss," or the "Networker," projecting an identity so that you can be as successful as possible and get the responses back that you're seeking. The problem is that we have all these unconscious behaviors that we're not aware of, and we're projecting all of that energy, too. That's our shadow energy, of which we might not be aware, but we project nonetheless. This shadow energy, along with the unconscious behaviors it entails, can trigger reactions from others, often attracting individuals who activate our triggers. For example, if you leave a job because of a frustrating boss, only to encounter a similar personality in a new position, it illustrates how we can unwittingly repeat patterns of interaction, responding in familiar ways to the same archetypal energies manifested by different individuals.

Ultimately, over time, you begin to realize that this individual, this boss who acts in a certain way and triggers you, also appears in different areas of your life. They might manifest as a family member who frequently triggers you or as someone in your community with a remarkably similar personality.

---

[27] Spitzer, Anais N., et al. "Archetype." *Encyclopedia of Psychology and Religion*, 2010, pp. 67–70, link.springer.com/referenceworkentry/10.1007%2F978-0-387-71802-6_45, https://doi.org/10.1007/978-0-387-71802-6_45.

The reason they trigger you is due to unresolved emotional issues you have not addressed, possibly without even realizing their existence. Each time you engage in this energetic exchange – this projection and reflection of energy – it creates this sort of negative tension, especially in office spaces. Most people are unaware of the underlying reasons, but it significantly impacts the environment, driven largely by our egos and a basic level of reactivity to our immediate surroundings. This situation is exacerbated by our tendency to bring our personal traumas to work. We are often expected to compartmentalize our personas, as if it were a literal requirement of our job descriptions.

The expectation is that we will arrive at work as highly logical individuals, focused and purposeful, completing our tasks, receiving our paychecks, and then departing to live our separate lives. This view might seem reasonable, except for the fact that we are human beings with interconnected emotions and intellect. Attempting to suppress either aspect leads to complications. We are incapable of true compartmentalization and are much more than just the sum of our triggers. Therefore, it's crucial for the corporate world to take a step back and look at the expectations placed on human beings working in a corporate environment. How can we transform the corporate environment from a space dominated by egos and survival mode into one filled with genuinely authentic individuals who are thriving, productive, and fully engaged in their work?

Action Items and Journal Prompts: Chapter 3

Reflections

- Are there places where you don't feel like you fit in? How do you act in those environments? Do you find yourself trying to adapt in order to be accepted or rebelling to stand out even more?

- Think about a time when you did something outside of "the norm." What inspired you, and how did you feel? Describe the experience.

- Who do you know or admire that has followed their own path? What can you learn from their journey?

- Do you think of yourself as more or less traditional? How are you judging that word?

- Does corporate culture feel inclusive to you? Expand on your feelings about this.

Actions

- **Get Uncomfortable.** Do something outside of your comfort zone at least once every month. Embrace a learning and experience mindset. These can be simple tasks, like making a meal that you judge as complicated, doing a creative project, or listening to an artist or watching a show in a genre you normally avoid. The key is to create new experiences for yourself and learn.

- **Learn a Different Skill.** Get certified in a skill that seems unrelated to your profession. How does it shift or expand your perspective?

CHAPTER 4

CULTURE MYTHS

"Creating the culture of burnout is the opposite of creating
a culture of sustainable creativity."
– Arianna Huffington, Founder of The Huffington Post

Similarly to how individuals have shadows and aspects of themselves that they conceal, I believe that companies possess shadows as well. I refer to these as "brand shadows," which occur in various ways within Corporate America. Many brand shadows exist that some wish to dismiss as myths or hope remain unnoticed, but some are gradually being revealed. The most significant shadow involves core values being non-existent or disregarded. When companies claim to uphold values that are absent, it reflects poorly on them. For example, it's more respectable for an organization to openly acknowledge its focus on profit above all rather than falsely professing to prioritize its people without actual commitment. We're at a crucial inflection point with respect to examining corporate values, with growing expectations from customers and employees for these values to be genuine, authentic, and actionable.

Defining Corporations

There are legal definitions for what a corporation is. It's a legal business structure. While there are variations in how a corporation can be organized, key defining elements include limited liability, organizational structure, regulatory compliance, and perpetual existence. Beyond the legal framework, there's a cultural understanding of what being "corporate" entails, signifying a particular business approach. This cultural definition extends beyond legally defined corporations, influencing many sectors that adopt corporate business practices without the legal structure, such as nonprofits, direct-to-consumer ventures, and various service organizations. One myth lies in the belief that the corporate way is the sole approach to conducting business, overlooking alternative models that eschew the traditional corporate framework.

A Holacracy is a decentralized system that is distributed and self-organizing. The focus is on agility and adaptability, and it's more of a circular structure than a hierarchical pyramid. Decision-making involves all aspects of the organization and is typically democratic. Organizations focused on innovation and creativity might prefer this structure to a traditional corporate structure because it promotes a balance of autonomy in decision-making with a culture of collaboration.

Flat organizations are similar, with little or no hierarchy, built around open communication channels and collaborative decision-making. The goal in these businesses is maximizing limited resources, so startups and nonprofits often adopt a flat structure.

There are also **Co-Operatives (Co-Ops)**, where members are a part of the decision-making process of the organization. Co-ops are usually value-driven or value-based, purpose-driven businesses and the members are considered owners.

There are social **Enterprises**, which have priorities beyond just the bottom line, where success is measured on the basis of other outcomes such as environmental impact or ethical expression.

Another expanding alternative to corporate culture is the gig economy and freelancers. The gig economy provides workers the freedom to work with multiple clients and make self-directed decisions. Freelancers can establish their own work structure and offer valuable skills, but they sacrifice job stability and the benefits often associated with traditional employment. However, data indicates a growing trend of freelancers finding security in diversifying their client base rather than depending on a single employer.[28] As portable benefits, or benefits that are tied to the worker instead of the employer, become more accessible, individuals will feel even less need to attach themselves to just one employer. This impacts everyone, especially organizations focused on employee retention and culture development.

With business practices in a state of constant change, clinging to a single model out of fear or a lack of vision is a limited approach. Embracing change and its potential allows for genuine growth. People will continue to devise new ways of doing business, both within and beyond traditional corporate frameworks. Examining and understanding the benefits and drawbacks of different business models is just one way that we can consider how to integrate alternatives and innovate business practices. There's no reason to adhere to outdated corporate practices, especially when they have become unsustainable or destructive. Corporate America has the opportunity to embrace change and evolve itself, but it will take a commitment from all levels.

Organizational Personas

Just as I mentioned, individuals have personas that we express, project, or even repress into our shadow; I believe companies have personas too. When discussing this, many might immediately think of company branding, which certainly plays a role. However, my concept of a "Company" persona

---

[28] Hansen, Megan. "Who Benefits from the Gig Economy?" James Madison Institute, 14 Mar. 2019, jamesmadison.org/who-benefits-from-the-gig-economy/.

transcends the traditional notion of branding. The brand, as it was previously understood, has evolved into a myth. The fundamental goal of a business is to solve a specific problem for a customer, whether that customer is an individual or another business. The nature of these problems can range from complex to simple, with solutions typically taking the form of services, products, experiences, or a blend of these elements.

For a long time, companies constructed highly curated and tightly controlled brands. If anything occurred that could tarnish the brand's image, many companies' initial reaction was to ensure it remained hidden. When secrecy was not possible, PR and risk management teams would get to work immediately to try to minimize the impact to the brand. And if all else failed, a company could always just rebrand, get a fresh new logo, and even change its name. For example, British Petroleum, also known as BP, spent over $210 million dollars rebranding after their disastrous Deepwater Horizon oil spill cost them more than $65B in fines and recovery costs.[29] They got a shiny new logo and put on a shiny new face. But the advent of the internet leveled the playing field for consumers and businesses alike, making a company's brand more transparent, whether the company wanted it or not. Consumers became vocal about their experiences, sharing reviews across social media platforms, and companies' responses came under greater scrutiny. Rebranding was no longer a straightforward escape; companies had to address their customers' concerns directly and in public forums, leading to a greater focus on customer experience, also known as CX.

Around 2007, something else happened that had a significant impact on brand management not only with customers but also with employees. A company called Glassdoor was founded, offering employees a public platform

---

[29] co, the cre8tive. "What We Can Learn from BP Rebranding." *Medium*, 8 Feb. 2020, medium.com/@thecre8tiveco/what-we-can-learn-from-bp-rebranding-4398c98d63c5#:~:text=BP%20spent%20%24211%20million%20on.

to anonymously rate and review their work experience. Glassdoor's basic premise allowed employees free site access in exchange for a single, anonymous review. Employees could evaluate the organization, salaries, culture, and leadership, and prospective employees could even review the interview process. As employee feedback accumulated, companies took notice. Glassdoor charged companies for brand management and administrative control over their pages, except for the reviews – Glassdoor maintains that no company can pay to remove negative reviews, which are only deleted if they violate the published standards. Glassdoor and similar platforms presented companies with a public evaluation tool that job seekers could leverage, making achieving and maintaining a rating of 3.0 or higher a goal for many HR departments as they worked to attract and retain talent.

The ways in which consumers and employees share their experiences had a dramatic impact on how companies began to see themselves. A crucial factor in how an organization conveys an authentic persona – making it relatable and connectable for its audience – relates to its values. A 2023 Forbes article mentioned that about 90% of companies have documented values or mission statements.[30] It also highlighted the challenges many organizations face in genuinely embodying these values and offered practical advice on how companies could better implement them. I think that many businesses face challenges when it comes to their values because they aren't thinking about how these values look in action. A company may say they value diversity and even believe it, but if leaders aren't creating mechanisms to activate that value throughout the business, they will struggle to express it. One thing the article suggests is testing out your values - are they values that can be upheld and expressed authentically? The values of customers and employees do not have to be completely aligned to the business, but they are looking for consistency

---

[30] Smith, Greg. "Council Post: Core Values Can Supercharge Your Creator Business: Here's How." *Forbes*, 24 Aug. 2023, www.forbes.com/sites/forbestechcouncil/2023/08/24/core-values-can-supercharge-your-creator-business-heres-how/?sh=523192f53f82.

and truth. This allows each person to reasonably negotiate their own values and determine if engaging with a particular brand will serve their needs.

Even still, the way that values are expressed in companies often feels contrived when they aren't driven by authentic actions from the highest levels. Leadership drives values, and misalignment can severely impact the brand. Misalignment often arises when leaders fail to exemplify the values they claim their company upholds. This discrepancy can be expressed in various ways, such as proclaiming the importance of valuing people but failing to invest in or care for employees in their times of need. Another example is tolerating poor or unethical behavior, contradicting a professed value of integrity. People notice and sense these inconsistencies within the culture. A culture that mandates obedience without question does not consider its impact on the workforce. Misaligned values can cause significant harm. Conversely, aligned values can strengthen the brand, something both customers and employees increasingly seek.[31] They want to know who they're doing business with, whether making purchases or working on their behalf; they want to know that they're being represented honestly and authentically.

As I am writing this, we have witnessed in real time a value misalignment occurring within a major company, Boeing. This misalignment has unfolded over a long period, as cultural shifts by nature do not happen overnight, especially in large companies where changes tend to occur more slowly. Boeing has experienced engineering failures in their last two major models, the 737 Max 8 and 737 Max 9. These failures resulted in the loss of lives and significant damage, impacting not just Boeing but the airline industry as a whole. The disregard for safety and lack of oversight have fostered fear and mistrust towards the airline industry.

---

[31] Adams, C. "Do Our Customers Really Care about Our Corporate Values?" *LinkedIn*, 14 Sep. 2022, www.linkedin.com/pulse/do-our-customers-really-care-corporate-values-chris-adams/.

Tragically, these incidents are not Boeing's first major failures resulting in death or trauma, but merely their most recent.[32] Boeing, established in 1916, has been known for over a century for its core values of engineering excellence and safety, claims that are still made on their website.[33] However, following their 1998 merger with McDonnell Douglas, many observed a shift from the company's traditional focus on engineering and safety to an emphasis on profitability and cost-cutting measures. This shift did not happen instantly but gradually became apparent, with early signs of significant trouble emerging as early as 2008. What we are observing now is the outcome of this value and cultural shift within a large, storied organization. Beyond the irreplaceable loss of lives and the trauma inflicted on families, the financial repercussions are tremendous. Still recovering from their crash scandals of 2018-2019, Boeing reported[34] a net loss of $2.2 billion during the first nine months of 2023, with further losses anticipated. The shift from prioritizing engineering excellence to focusing on profit and operational efficiencies may have yielded short-term benefits for some, but has proven to be detrimental in the long run.

The Human Resources Dilemma

"HR is Not Your Friend." I used this statement as a hook on a reel I posted to Instagram, and it sparked a lot of disruption and division. Although it seemed direct and perhaps subjective to many, my intention was not to attack HR professionals but rather to comment on HR's positioning within many companies. I hold sincere respect for HR professionals and understand

---

[32] Syme, Pete. "Boeing's Quality-Control Process and Company Culture Are Being Heavily Scrutinized after the 737 Max Flight 1282 Blowout." *Business Insider*, Jan. 2024, www.businessinsider.com/boeing-737-max-quality-control-company-culture-merger-finances-2024-1#.

[33] Boeing, "Values." www.boeing.com/sustainability/values.

[34] Cooban, A. "Boeing Stock Plunges after a Piece of Fuselage on a Boeing 737 Max 9 Blew out Mid-Flight." *6ABC Philadelphia*, 8 Jan. 2024, 6abc.com/boeing-stock-price-737-9-max/14296201/#:~:text=Since%20the%20grounding%20of%20the.

the complex requirements and expectations of their roles. The myth surrounding HR culture is that many companies place HR departments in difficult positions, depending on whether organizational values are effectively demonstrated by leadership. If HR plays a significant role within leadership, then the outcomes and experiences for employees, as well as the overall culture, are significantly improved. However, in a toxic culture where HR lacks authority and is positioned differently by leadership, this creates mistrust and confusion among employees. Such situations put enormous pressure on HR staff, who typically enter the field with a desire to assist people. When they are not empowered to enforce values and are expected to shield leadership from the fallout of toxic behaviors, it not only harms HR professionals personally but also tarnishes the perception of the department as a whole.

I have spoken to many people who describe their negative experiences with HR in personal terms. Generally, employees may describe personal or emotional experiences with their boss or another colleague, but HR is the only department that consistently comes up in this manner. Few people leave an organization feeling betrayed by IT or Marketing. One theory is that employees may anthropomorphize a company, or view it as a human, and in doing so, they see HR practices in the same way they perceive the behaviors and actions of an individual.[35] In this way, HR is expressing the organizational culture on behalf of the entire company.

The department of human resources is tasked with understanding and enforcing the guidelines, rules, and regulations necessary for an organization to maintain proper, legal business practices, particularly regarding people and their employment. This broad definition encompasses myriad responsibilities,

---

[35] Wang, Ying, et al. "Employee Perceptions of HR Practices: A Critical Review and Future Directions." *The International Journal of Human Resource Management*, vol. 31, no. 1, 26 Nov. 2019, pp. 128–173, https://doi.org/10.1080/09585192.2019.1674360.

including recruiting and retention of staff, creating benefit packages, determining salary structures, and setting organizational guidelines for employees. HR responsibilities range from handling tedious regulatory work to providing staff training and education, supporting cultural initiatives like organizing holiday gatherings and employee events and conducting exit interviews and layoffs. Most importantly, every time you get paid on time, you can thank your HR department. It's a significant burden for a single department, and it's understandable how this could lead to confusion among employees. This confusion can escalate to mistrust and even anger towards HR in toxic workplaces, where HR often seems to be in the position of protecting leadership at the expense of an employee's well-being, or even their job. In toxic cultures, HR frequently navigates value misalignments and delicate situations, bearing the responsibility for many aspects of organizational culture.

The HR professionals I work with describe the pressure of navigating their roles and the emotions that arise. Almost universally, they express a desire to improve situations and help others.

Signs indicate that trends in HR are shifting for the betterment of employees and the health of businesses, but these changes will take time to permeate corporate culture. A recent report[36] showed that among Fortune 200 companies, 187 had Chief Human Resource Officers (CHROs), granting HR a crucial seat at the leadership table. Not only are more companies appointing CHROs, but they are also enhancing their compensation. This progressive view of HR addresses issues strategically, aligns values, and demonstrates that culture can evolve in intentional, organic ways, marking a significant shift in how companies perceive HR and its strategic leadership impact. The focus is

---

[36] Heilferty, Annarose. "CHRO Trends 2022 Report." The Talent Strategy Group, 13 July 2022, talentstrategygroup.com/chro-trends-2022-report/#:~:text=In%20total%2C%20187%20of%20the.

increasingly on the "human" element rather than merely the "resources" aspect.

However, many companies, particularly smaller ones, may not be able to afford a CHRO. In these organizations, HR may not be strategically implemented, often growing from within and viewed by many leaders as administrative rather than strategic. HR practices develop as an extension of existing leadership practices, or sometimes, companies adapt HR practices as they expand. Over time, HR finds itself reacting to the needs of leadership and the company. Yet, when conflicts arise or employees face issues, HR is caught in the middle, contributing to the negative perceptions and spread of toxic culture.

For a period of time,[37] companies appeared to try addressing this problem by separating corporate resources from cultural resources and creating Chief Culture Officers, or CCOs. I can see how businesses could see this as beneficial in organizations. The logic goes something like this: "If we just kept all of the compliance and regulatory needs of HR in one place, and created a separate culture department that focuses on employee advocacy, building culture, training, employee development, then it would solve these issues." But this is like saying that building more roads will reduce traffic. It doesn't get to the core issue. If leadership drives culture, then a department focused on culture will in some ways create more disconnection. Leadership has to embrace and model the values of the organization, and when they do, it becomes easy for departmental leaders across the organization to do the same. When this occurs, employees feel this continuity and connection to the organization. Everyone, including employees, should be empowered to

---

[37] Clayton, Neil Barman and Sarah Jensen. "The Chief Culture Officer Role Is Quickly Disappearing." *Quartz*, 31 Aug. 2023, qz.com/the-chief-culture-officer-role-is-quickly-disappearing-1850789015.

express and contribute to the company culture, but they have to understand it and believe in it for that to happen.

Toxic by Design

On some level, there exists a myth about business ethics that no one seems to want to address: when the ends and the means are misaligned, it cannot be considered "good business." It appears that toxic culture is, at times, intentionally cultivated. We've witnessed plenty of individuals build businesses that were never intended to have any socially good purpose, and so be it – in a purely capitalistic system, there is no requirement for social benefit. But thinking about unscrupulous and unethical people like Bernie Madoff, for example, is illuminating. Madoff defrauded tens of thousands, deceiving customers, employees, and families, and died in prison. While these are the actions of an individual who ultimately paid for his crime, I think it's worth considering the system that enabled figures like Madoff. Jordan Belfort, the subject of the film *The Wolf of Wall Street* (discussed above), is a similar figure. Belfort, having profited from his crimes, boasts a net worth of around $115M.[38] In 2023, he made a return to the financial services industry, and is once again asking people to place their trust in him.

When reflecting on individuals and corporations like Enron or BP, driven solely by profit without regard for customers or employees, the destructive impact of business toxicity becomes starkly evident. These cases resulted in widespread harm, including financial ruin for many and significant social and environmental damage. Leaders of socially toxic organizations have also made headlines for creating demoralizing work environments while violating ethical standards and laws. A prominent

---

[38] Greenberg, Gregg. "Jordan Belfort is Back on Wall Street and Talking with InvestmentNews." *InvestmentNews*, 2 Nov. 2023, https://www.investmentnews.com/investing/news/jordan-belfort-is-back-on-wall-street-and-talking-with-investmentnews-245197.

example is Elizabeth Holmes of Theranos, the youngest self-made billionaire,[39] and also turned criminal. Holmes and co-leader Ramesh Balwani compromised all integrity in pursuit of their vision, endangering and harming people in the process. The more committed they were to the lie, the more the toxicity of her organization bled out, making it harder and harder to conceal. The astonishing aspect of the Theranos story was how many respected and known leaders were so invested in the vision that they overlooked obvious signs of distress and allowed this toxic organization to perpetuate itself. Business shouldn't cause harm in order to thrive, but it often does. We need to consider the influence these types of situations have on the wider culture. These are all examples of corporate shadows.

Toxic Cycles

While I believe that some toxic companies are intentionally created, most toxic cultures arise accidentally, not by design. Toxic cultures start in a variety of ways, but almost always stem from leadership. One example of this is when businesses can't make a transition from the startup phase and into the growth phase, where they begin building a team, and by default, their culture.

It looks something like this: Early on in that startup phase, you have a small group working together (sometimes just two or three people), and they're all very focused on a vision and a purpose. They're very connected through that vision and purpose, and in that context, they're likely tolerating idiosyncrasies or behavior patterns of each other that, in that small setting, are not necessarily toxic. They may be behaviors that need to be addressed and which call for boundaries to be set early on, but they're manageable, or not worth the cost, so they get ignored. And they continue to be manageable until

---

[39] Hart, Robert. "Elizabeth Holmes – Theranos Fraudster and Ex-Billionaire – Gets Two Years Cut from off Prison Sentence." *Forbes*, 11 July 2023, www.forbes.com/sites/roberthart/2023/07/11/elizabeth-holmes-theranos-fraudster-and-ex-billionaire-quietly-cuts-two-years-off-prison-sentence/?sh=751b7fbb2836.

the environment outgrows them. This is because, while they are aligned on the vision, they haven't aligned on other important aspects of the business, such as the culture and values they want to express. Occasionally, aspects of this are addressed during a branding exercise, but not to the extent that leaders understand the enormity of the transition they will need to make. One article suggested that as many as 65% of startups fail due to misalignment of leaders.[40]

This becomes more apparent as companies grow beyond ten to twenty people, moving towards fifty. At this stage, the culture begins to expand, and behaviors that were once considered innocuous or manageable by a few become the cultural standard. Misalignments turn into chasms that fragment the culture and disrupt the business. Without established accountability from the start, leaders are not taught how to transition from being an entrepreneur to being an actual leader, which requires a completely different mindset.

Beyond misaligned leaders, toxic cultures develop when companies fail to make their values known and actionable. As mentioned earlier, although 90% of companies have documented values, they often fail to strategically implement these values in meaningful ways. They also fail to empower employees to embody these values, leading to stagnation and, over time, further misalignment or complete loss of these values. Active values, such as "we value people," can directly contribute to the bottom line, making it more or less profitable depending on the commitment to these values.

A Gallup study from 2019 reported that US companies lost one trillion dollars in a single year due to voluntary employee turnover.[41] As staggering as

---

[40] Conlan, Bryce. "Harvard Business School Professor Says 65% of Startups Fail for One Reason. Here's How to Avoid It." *Entrepreneur*, 8 June 2021, www.entrepreneur.com/leadership/harvard-business-school-professor-says-65-of-startups-fail/370367.

[41] McFeely, Shane, and Ben Wigert. "This Fixable Problem Costs U.S. Businesses $1 Trillion." *Gallup*, 13 Mar. 2019, www.gallup.com/workplace/247391/fixable-problem-costs-businesses-trillion.aspx.

that figure is, it becomes even more alarming when broken down to reflect its impact on smaller organizations. The study found that for every employee a company loses, it costs, on average, two and a half times their salary to replace them. For a company of 100 people, based on voluntary employee turnover, the costs were estimated to range from $600,000 to over $2.5 million a year, accounting for lost revenue, training, time investments, experience, and intellectual knowledge. Considering this data alongside another study showing that toxic culture is more than ten times more likely to cause an employee to leave than compensation issues, it's clear this is an expensive problem that cannot be ignored.[42] The real cost of not establishing clear values and allowing your culture to become toxic enough to drive such turnover is immense.

Another aspect often overlooked in examinations of corporate culture is that the absence of clearly established values makes it easier to accept mediocrity. This helps explain why there are many poorly trained managers. People are promoted to leadership positions, where they should be elevating or guiding others, without being equipped with the necessary skills. This lack of skill set often stems from being promoted by someone who also lacked these abilities, creating a cycle of tolerating mediocrity and becoming increasingly mediocre. Without upholding or modeling expectations for excellence, "good enough" becomes the standard.

One such scenario of tolerating poor behavior is allowing your "Big Ass Producer" (BAP) to be emotionally abusive or reactive to staff. The BAP gets away with creating an environment of disrespect, and this is tolerated because of the productivity that's happening in the immediate moment. The

---

[42] Sull, Donald, et al. "Toxic Culture Is Driving the Great Resignation." *MIT Sloan Management Review*, 11 Jan. 2022, sloanreview.mit.edu/article/toxic-culture-is-driving-the-great-resignation/.

organization chooses to ignore the long-term ramifications and impact of that one individual and the energy that they're bringing into that environment.

Microcultures and Silos

Are all silos bad, or are some of them just self-preserving? I find microcultures within toxic organizations fascinating. They can be either beneficial or detrimental. A microculture can certainly lead to silos or emerge as a result of them. I've observed microcultures that formed healthy teams or departments, where a strong manager created a buffer environment that allowed their team to remain productive. This often places the manager in the challenging position of managing both upwards and downwards.

I once experienced this myself. I was building a new team in a conservative environment, which I'd describe as a quiet place – a hushed landscape of gray cubicles filled with serious, sad workers. I'm being only slightly hyperbolic. I was building a new marketing team and we all loved our jobs. As the team expanded, we implemented new and efficient processes, developed engaging collateral, and forged strong cross-departmental relationships. Things seemed to be progressing exceptionally well for us.

Then, one day, I was called into the office of the senior VP of the department, my boss's boss, someone I respected highly at the time and still do today. "Stephanie, I know you're developing your team," she began. "You're doing a kick-ass job. I can see the work that you're doing. We see what you all are producing, and you're exceeding expectations. But, we're getting a lot of complaints about your team." I immediately asked what the complaints were. Her response was awkward for both of us. She understood how her feedback was going to come across. She told me the complaints were that we were enjoying our jobs too openly.

"You're... you're expressing too much joy," she said. As she expected, I didn't understand the feedback.

"Are we being disruptive?" I asked.

She told me no, that's not the reason she'd gotten the complaint. She said that "people hear your team working together and collaborating, and they don't understand how you can be so productive and enjoy your job so much." So, in essence, we were being disruptive in that culture because sometimes we laughed when we were working. Right then, I learned a lot about the culture that I was already in. I knew that I had been buffering my team, but I didn't realize how much until then. I had to go back to them and give them that feedback. It was my job to let everybody know what the expectations were.

It can be difficult to tell a group of people you're trying to keep in a creative and innovative headspace, "We need to tone down how much we're expressing joy." However, my approach is usually to be truthful, so I shared the feedback and we brainstormed it. As weird as the initial feedback felt, we understood that many of our colleagues had very focused jobs, where even quiet conversation might be disruptive. Our work often depended on collaboration, and we were a new department. We wanted to respect the existing culture and also find a way to immediately raise our awareness. Someone on the team suggested the phrase "dead puppies." We all agreed it was the most joyless phrase we could come up with. For a while, that became our safe word for excessive joy. If we started giggling or getting too engrossed in our collaborations, someone would mention "dead puppies," and we would all go silent. It was a piece of morbid humor, but it was our way of dealing with a situation that felt, in some ways, more severe.

As a manager, I began negotiating for a new workspace for my team, where we could collaborate freely without causing disruption. It was only a few months before we moved, allowing us to retire our phrase. Until that point, it had never occurred to me that enjoying our work could be problematic. Although we respected the feedback, it was still difficult to rationalize being told that we were expressing too much joy.

Female Non Grata (or FNG)

I am a woman who has worked in primarily male-dominated corporate environments for many years, and I've greatly enjoyed that work. I've worked with many exceptional men who have both championed and challenged me, and I've learned a lot from them. I've also had experiences in corporate spaces that I hope others never have to endure, but I'm certain many have.

While progress has occurred over the years, the myth that women are fully welcomed in corporate spaces persists. Women bring a unique energy and authority; we embody our own strength and power. This may not resemble how traditional corporate strength and power have been projected in the past, but it is no less valuable. We're still working in the shadows of the "Me Too" movement, which has significantly impacted and raised awareness – an awareness that continues to grow. However, it often feels as though the corporate world has resisted giving up perceived power to women. In response, women have been taking that control in their own ways. More women are starting their businesses, achieving remarkable success.

A Wells Fargo market study published this year indicated that from 2019 to 2023, businesses owned by women saw growth outpacing men's businesses by over 94%.[43] Women are no longer content to wait for a seat at an overcrowded conference table with a group of men who see them as a threat instead of an asset. Instead, they are carving out paths of independence and empowerment by establishing the types of businesses they wish they could have worked for. Another noteworthy finding from the study is that during the pandemic, women-owned businesses accounted for 1.4 million jobs. It seems Corporate America is beginning to catch up; in 2023, for the first time

---

[43] Wells Fargo & Company. "New Report Finds Growth of Women Business Owners Outpaces the Market." *Wells Fargo Newsroom*, 9 Jan. 2024, https://newsroom.wf.com/English/news-releases/news-release-details/2024/New-Report-Finds-Growth-of-Women-Business-Owners-Outpaces-the-Market/.

in its nearly 70-year history, women constituted more than 10% of CEOs leading Fortune 500 companies.[44]

Did DEI Die?

Diversity, equity, and inclusion (DEI) initiatives are reportedly facing their demise, according to several recent reports,[45] with organizations scaling back their investments in these programs almost as swiftly as they increased them in 2020 following George Floyd's death. But is this truly happening, and what implications does it have for corporate culture? As DEI practices become increasingly politicized – evidenced by states like Texas and Florida even going so far as to pass laws barring these types of initiatives – up to 79% of HR leaders in one study[46] claimed they remain committed to the practices they implemented over the past few years. There are clear indicators that these initiatives were making a difference, with Bloomberg[47] reporting that out of over 300,000 jobs created in 2023, approximately 94% were filled by people of color. This statistic leads some to speculate that the recent backlash may be a reaction to these significant strides in workplace diversity.

Not all DEI programs are the same. Some are more effective than others, and when they are successful, the impact and results are felt throughout the organization. Programs that foster a genuine culture of trust and transparency

---

[44] Hinchcliffe, E. "Women Run More than 10% of Fortune 500 Companies for the First Time." *Www.shrm.org*, 30 Jan. 2023, www.shrm.org/executive-network/insights/women-run-10-fortune-500-companies-first-time#:~:text=Now%2C%20for%20the%20first%20time.

[45] Peck. E. "Companies Are Backing Away from 'DEI'." *Axios*, 4 Jan. 2024, https://www.axios.com/2024/01/04/dei-jobs-diversity-corporate.

[46] Soutar, L. "'Real Implications': Huge Majority of HR Leaders Agree D&I Crucial for Business Performance." *HR Grapevine*, 10 Aug. 2023, https://www.hrgrapevine.com/content/article/2023-08-09-huge-majority-of-hr-leaders-agree-di-crucial-for-business-performance.

[47] Green, Jeff, et al. "Corporate America Promised to Hire a Lot More People of Color. It Actually Did." *Bloomberg.com*, 25 Sept. 2023, www.bloomberg.com/graphics/2023-black-lives-matter-equal-opportunity-corporate-diversity/.

and engage with customers and employees to learn from them are more successful in developing and implementing DEI initiatives. Intel is one organization that has made significant strides in its DEI efforts by undertaking visible and impactful actions such as setting and achieving the goal of spending $1 billion with diverse suppliers and committing to diverse mentorship and leadership programs.[48]

As the political climate surrounding this issue intensifies, business leaders must decide what is most profitable and what will generate the most long-term value for their companies. Cultivating diversity, equity, and inclusion within an organization broadens the talent pool by creating an environment where everyone can work and thrive safely. It's also important to note that values-driven Gen Z expects employers to prioritize DEI, and their commitment to these values could significantly influence their ability to attract Gen Z talent.[49]

We're All Replaceable

Another cultural myth is the notion that everyone is replaceable. You can devote a tremendous amount of hard work and effort, only to be suddenly devalued and dismissed, often in many states without cause. Running a business based on fear, which keeps employees in survival mode, undermines workforce morale, and fundamentally devalues people. However, not everyone is replaceable. I think that's bullshit, and it should be called out that way. Sometimes, people are only replaceable with five other people, which says a lot about what was being put on that person's plate to begin with. The concept of everybody being replaceable is a real brand shadow that leads right

---

[48] Jay, Shani. "13 Tried-And-Tested DEI Initiatives to Implement [in 2023]." *AIHR*, 17 July 2023, www.aihr.com/blog/dei-initiatives/.

[49] INOP, "Gen Z Workforce: Values as the Catalyst for Job Change." *LinkedIn*, 1 June 2023, www.linkedin.com/pulse/gen-z-workforce-values-catalyst-job-change-inop-ai/.

into fear-based management: surviving and not thriving, not having a "work-life" balance, and enabling managers to intimidate staff.

Companies that fail to value or respect employees' personal time and ignore the significant impact this has on their mental health are contributing to this problem. One study found that 69% of employees identified their manager as having the most significant impact on their personal mental health, more than anybody else in their life, including their doctor or spouse/significant other.[50] This is because employees spend a considerable amount of time working with or around their manager, who wields considerable influence over their lives, including their income, career growth, upward mobility, and employment status.

Many of these culture myths are very difficult realities that Corporate America needs to find a way to address. There are also ways individuals can challenge these myths and their own beliefs surrounding them. We each have our own conditioning and bias that keeps us from seeing possibilities. As we increase our awareness, we are able to see where change can and should happen, and most importantly, why.

---

[50] Brower, T. "Managers Have Major Impact on Mental Health: How to Lead for Wellbeing." *Forbes*, 29 Jan. 2023, www.forbes.com/sites/tracybrower/2023/01/29/managers-have-major-impact-on-mental-health-how-to-lead-for-wellbeing/?sh=6e038ec92ec1.

Action Items and Journal Prompts: Chapter 4

Reflections

- When you think about your company, either as a leader or an employee, in what ways could you see it functioning differently to improve the culture?

- Have you experienced any of the culture myths discussed here? How have they impacted your perspective of your work and career?

- What does transparency mean to you? How transparent are you in your personal life versus your professional life?

- Does your company brand have a shadow or some aspect that it tries to hide?

- How do you feel about the idea that people are replaceable? How do you feel about yourself being replaceable? Examine these feelings.

Actions

- **Empower Yourself.** Whether you're an employee or manager, take time to understand the following:
  - The Equal Employment Opportunity Commission (EEOC) https://www.eeoc.gov/employers/small-business/employee-rights
  - Your state's labor laws and legal assistance resources
  - The resources available within your organization

- **Empower Others.** The best way to help empower others is by empowering yourself first, then sharing the knowledge. As a leader, this should come naturally to you.

CHAPTER 5

GAMIFYING THE SYSTEM

"No individual can win a game by himself."
– Pelé, Brazilian Professional Footballer, *"World Face of Soccer"*

As discussed earlier, I first came into the corporate world via a non-traditional route. I entered the corporate world through sales, and I was an exceptional salesperson. I did very well in that role and learned a great deal about business and my own skills and motivations. As I developed, I was able to get training and enough education to move into marketing, which I saw as more creative and which felt like a better fit. Though I still lacked a formal degree, I had gained real-world experience, began my educational pursuits, and proven my abilities.

From a very early stage, my perspective was to view the corporate world as a game space. It wasn't a stretch for me to see it this way. I participated in the world of analog gaming during a time when I was often the only girl at the table, playing games like D&D and Magic: The Gathering. Many of the gaming concepts and strategies we used layered nicely over the corporate system and how it worked. I believed that my role in the game, in this corporate RPG, was to be a Good Corporate Citizen. I had a certain mistrust for this world, and that was the role that I believed would help me advance and level up. I wanted to do good things. I wanted to show that I had the right work ethic, express integrity, and hone my capacity to expand and lead. I also needed to learn humility and the ability to not always be right. I worked hard to objectively examine how I could continually learn and improve myself. For me, this was the criteria that I would use to become a Good Corporate Citizen.

Looking back at my younger, idealist self, I know that much of this was survival mode. I was creating a defense mechanism to cover up the imposter syndrome that I felt for not having all the traditional things. When I looked at the corporate system as a game, it made it easier for me to figure out how to navigate and what I was supposed to do there. I could compartmentalize myself in that space. I could figure out how to level up or advance in that space. I also learned what my degree of value negotiation was in that context and where I had boundaries or limitations.

In a gaming environment, there are things that you have to know and understand as you're building your game strategy. One of the first things you do is choose your role – the persona you want to play. In choosing the persona of the Good Corporate Citizen, I also had to define it for myself. I had to decide: How am I going to show up? Who am I in this world? I showed up as an outspoken, creative person who appeared fearless in many ways. I showed up as a very independent-minded, innovative thinker. I had to learn how to take criticism and offer productive feedback. I learned how to listen to other people's ideas and to problem-solve non-creative challenges in very creative ways. This was all a natural fit for my innate skills and personality, and for a long time, this persona allowed me to grow and expand. Eventually, I was able to evolve into expressing myself authentically with less self-doubt. Like any avid gamer, with each new experience, I was intentionally manifesting what would come next.

Corporate Persona Archetypes

There are hundreds, if not thousands of different archetypes. At any given time, we can each express these archetypes or access the universal energy of an archetype. Many of us naturally gravitate towards a particular persona, but it helps to understand how all archetypal energy impacts us. In exploring the world of archetypes, I developed some essential corporate personas that I believe are universal to Corporate America. In total, I have created over fifty archetypes relating to the corporate world, and from these, I created a "Corporate Archetype" Persona Test using six specific archetypes: the "Big Boss," the "Office Parent," the "Analyzer," the "Creative," the "Networker," and the "Entrepreneur."

Let's explore these six primary corporate archetypes in more detail.

The "Office Parent"

The "Office Parent" often gets stereotyped in negative ways, and I have had people become upset with me when it came up as their result on my archetype quiz, primarily because of the stereotype that they also perceived. Based on the current data I have from my Persona Archetype Test, 28% of the respondents are projecting "Office Parent" energy. This is the largest group, so there are many of them out there. My experience with "Office Parent" personas is that they're often optimistic people who nurture and promote productivity and energy to the benefit of the environment. The "Office Parent" is getting their needs met in the corporate space by making sure that everybody else's needs are met.

For example, this is the person who knows that Fred has a late night on Wednesdays and is always going to come in grumpy on a Thursday morning, so they do something to mitigate that scenario. "Office Parents" know it's important to honor people when something special is happening in their life, or they deserve recognition. The shadow aspects of the "Office Parent" persona show up in a few ways. The stereotype is of a busybody or a people-pleaser, a person who is working to get their emotional needs met in the wrong places. As with many stereotypes, there's an element of truth to this, but it doesn't reveal the deeper truth, which is that the "Office Parent" can be acting out by avoiding or neglecting their own needs to take care of other people. Doing this repeatedly can create internal resentment and a victim mentality. Exploring the emotions at the root of this will help the "Office Parent" learn to set clear boundaries, prioritize self-care, and expand other aspects of their personalities.

The "Big Boss"

We've all known a "Big Boss" personality, even if they weren't the actual boss. "Big Bosses" make up the second largest cohort of respondents to my test at 26.2%, and I work with a lot of people who are challenged by the shadow aspects of this persona. The "Big Boss" seems to effortlessly project an air of authority. You know when you meet them that they have the capacity to lead. "Big Bosses" are usually direct, and they get things done. They are visionaries who see the big picture and they're able to create consensus to move things forward. A shadow aspect of the "Big Boss" energy is they can be disconnected from what's going on around them, even when they have a lot of influence. If the "Big Boss" is in a leadership position, this disconnection from the organizational culture that they're creating can have serious effects. If the "Big Boss" isn't modeling organizational values, or only expressing authoritarian behavior, they can easily create a toxic culture of mistrust, intimidation, and fear. Even so, while the "Big Boss" is naturally authoritative, they are capable of feeling and expressing empathy for the people they lead.

The "Analyzer"

Coming in at 14% of the cohort is the "Analyzer." "Analyzers" are driven by logic. They love data, numbers, and information. The "Analyzer" persona will sometimes align with the Myers-Briggs personality type of ISTJ (Introvert, Sensing, Thinking, Judging), and they're likely to be more focused on observing and examining information than on building relationships.

"Analyzers" make great problem-solvers who notice patterns, details, and data that others would overlook. One shadow aspect of the "Analyzer" is that they get analysis paralysis, or they get stuck in the data. "Analyzers" also sometimes struggle with emotional ambiguity or nuanced behaviors. Because of their nature, it's difficult for them to form a conclusion on the basis of limited information.

The "Entrepreneur"

Our fourth group, containing 13.7% of the respondents, are "Entrepreneurs." In an earlier chapter, I described "Entrepreneurs" and how and why I believe they enter into corporate environments. When an "Entrepreneur" persona type is a good fit for an environment that is capable of nurturing their needs, this persona will evolve in the "Innovator" archetype, serving as a creative problem solver. They are willing to ask questions and take risks for the betterment of improving things, be it products, processes, experiences, or even culture. I intentionally tested for "Entrepreneurs" instead of innovators because with more people becoming entrepreneurs combined with the gig economy, this persona feels important to understand. Shadow aspects of this persona can look like taking on too much work and an inability to delegate. By nature, "Entrepreneurs" are independent thinkers.

The "Networker"

Barely trailing behind the "Entrepreneur" cohort in my study is the "Networker" with 13.4% identifying with this persona energy. "Networkers" are, by nature, adaptable people who find it easy to connect with other people. More than just making connections, "Networkers" are highly resourceful, and capable of leveraging their networks to access information, resources, opportunities, and valuable contacts. They are excellent communicators and skilled relationship builders, and they often display a higher level of professional visibility than their non-networking peers. "Networkers" run into trouble when they overextend themselves. This can create burnout when they don't take the time to replenish and avoid networking fatigue. Another shadow for "Networkers" is having a hidden agenda or the perception that their relationships aren't authentic. A genuine interest in others and a willingness to offer support and value within their network will lead to more fruitful and rewarding connections.

The "Creative"

Finally, we come to "Creatives," who are by far my lowest response cohort, with only 4.7% of submitters identifying with this persona archetype. This makes me wonder if "Creatives" don't like taking personality tests or if they simply feel less welcomed in corporate spaces. When I took my own test, I scored very high as a "Creative" – 37% to be exact. It just means that I am comfortable expressing and projecting myself in creative ways, and for me, this is accurate. I have worked with many "Creatives" inside and outside of corporate spaces. One thing that seems universal from my experience is that someone who identifies as "Creative" rarely feels nurtured, supported, or even understood. The "Creative" persona archetype also expresses shadow characteristics that make it more difficult to assimilate easily into corporate spaces. Some of these characteristics include sensitivity to criticism, disorganization, and a resistance to the commercialization of their creative work. Building resilience to criticism, seeking constructive feedback, and finding a balance between creative exploration and practicality can help creatives harness their full potential and adapt better to corporate culture.

As I said, these are just a few of hundreds of persona archetypes, but some are more common, and it is helpful to have a perspective of what role you're playing in any environment: the energy you are projecting into a situation, what triggers you, and what gets pushed into your shadow. Most people are an amalgamation of many personas. The goal is to understand so you can integrate and access more energy and resources.

Leveling Up

College came later in my adult years, and so, for me, leveling up in business was about acquiring skills at each stage of business that I worked in. I approached each job as a master's course degree, wanting to learn and absorb as much as I could in each role. Through my experiences and professional growth, I have developed masterful knowledge in executive sales and consultative sales training. I did so by first working as an inside sales representative, then pursuing technical certifications, product sales certifications, executive sales training, and mentoring until I had developed into an enterprise-level sales executive.

One month, I earned enough commission to pay cash for a new car, and I consistently led in sales productivity while being a strong team player and celebrating the wins of my colleagues. I have expert knowledge in building and executing marketing strategy, operational marketing tools and processes, and exceptionally talented marketing teams. I have practiced and earned master's course knowledge in producing curriculums to train and develop people. I can build processes that solve problems and allow workflow, development, and productivity to occur smoothly and easily. These are all skills I acquired on the job. In most cases, I was offered opportunities that were mine to either accept or decline.

On one occasion I received a promotion that I wasn't expecting. I had been hired as a graphic designer and was really excited to work for this company in this role. It was about two months into the job, and I had been setting up processes for managing my projects because none existed. There wasn't a marketing team at the time, so my boss came to me and said, "We think you're doing a great job." The "we" was him and his boss, who would become my new boss. They wanted to make me a Communications Manager. By that stage of my career, I had worked in marketing jobs and sales jobs, but I had never held a position with the title "Communications Manager." It may seem ridiculous, but one night, in the pre-Amazon era, I went to a bookstore and searched for a "Communications Manager for Dummies" book. I genuinely did because I didn't know what was expected of me in this role, and I was afraid to ask and reveal my ignorance. I realized that these people saw skills in me and believed I was qualified for it, and I needed to ensure I met their expectations. While I didn't find the book I was looking for, I stepped into the role and embraced the new responsibilities as they came. I quickly learned to ask questions and seek out answers from multiple sources. Gaining perspective gave me what I needed to succeed. I didn't realize that in many ways I was already doing the job I was being promoted to, but I figured it out and was promoted eight more times in eight years. Each promotion provided me with experience, insight, and transformative challenges that propelled me forward.

When I talk about gaming the corporate experience, I don't mean it at all pejoratively. It's the best analogy I have to describe my way of leveling up in Corporate America. I'm learning at every level and integrating that knowledge and experience as I go. I've frequently accepted challenges that I've never confronted before, which may sound ridiculous to some, but it shows that I don't shy away from opportunities simply because I lack prior experience. I'm smart enough to recognize there are certain experiences I'm simply not qualified for, and I don't pretend to be. But I also learned early on that when someone sees potential in you, you should be willing to recognize it, too.

Another way I leveled up in my career was by leading at every level, leading from where I was at. This doesn't mean that I was the boss or tried to control every environment I was in; that's not what leading is about. Having grown up playing softball and loving team sports, I greatly value the experience of being on a team and being a team member. However, even as a team member, you should lead and model the behavior and standards you want to see around you. Thus, at every level of the organization, whether I was in an entry-level position or a leader responsible for other employees, I always approached my work with a leadership mentality, along with the accountability and responsibility that comes with it. I believe that's a key characteristic of leadership. It's not about controlling others or wielding power and authority. It's about aligning vision, talent, and energy in a way that enables us to succeed and vibrate at a higher frequency. This brings me to another key aspect of leveling up: learning and knowing your values.

As you level up in business, you make value-based choices throughout the process. There have been times in my professional life when I've had to make decisions based on my values, where my values were in conflict, and I had to decide: Is this the right place for me? Is it time for me to move on? Whenever necessary, I always make those decisions proactively. I know myself well enough to realize that once I sense my values have been compromised, I will inevitably bring about the end of that situation in one way or another. Rather than being passive and potentially leaving the company in a manner that leaves me dissatisfied, I choose to be proactive and make the decision to move on, sometimes taking steps back to advance. Many people argue that they can't take such a risk, and I don't judge others' choices in this regard. Everyone has to make decisions that work for them, but in my experience, ignoring a conflict of values can diminish your spirit, costing more than just a paycheck. It can affect your productivity, capacity for growth, and even your health. There's a real cost to staying in a position too long when you know it's time to leave.

Surviving and thriving in the corporate world involves knowing and growing your resources. There are various strategies for doing this, but understanding the culture you're in is the first and most important step. When people enter new jobs, whether stepping into a leadership position or any role within the organization, it is vital to be observant at the beginning. Pay attention to the dynamics of the organization, noting where energy flows and where blockages occur. Viewing your role through the lens of the value you aim to add to the company, you can identify opportunities to maximize your impact. An external perspective in a corporate setting can be incredibly valuable, and there's a brief window of opportunity to leverage this before you fully assimilate into the culture. You might identify needs and develop processes to alleviate pain points, enhance communication, or increase efficiency. Additionally, being new gives you the chance to act as a connector, especially in siloed environments. One of the most valuable actions I took in my business career was reaching out to other department leaders to understand their operations. Even if it didn't directly relate to my responsibilities, gaining insight into the broader workings of my company made me more effective in my role and a better collaborator with my colleagues.

I once worked for a company in a highly regulated environment, requiring both compliance and legal oversight for nearly everything we produced in marketing. The culture towards compliance was almost hostile, with people actively trying to circumvent compliance review because they felt it slowed down processes and impeded their creative freedom. Coming from very non-regulated environments, this was new to me. Initially, I couldn't understand why everyone was so frustrated. Then, I began to grasp the situation and its challenges when I received a "completed" marketing piece back from compliance, with edits necessitating a complete rewrite and redesign, causing us to miss a hard deadline. Instead of becoming angry, I took the time to understand the distinction between compliance and legal, for example, and the significance of these roles in a regulatory environment.

Once I understood their responsibilities, needs, and their impact on my work, I offered to collaborate to develop new processes. These processes included creating a compliance lexicon for language that would always be flagged and implementing a review and sign-off process before content ever went to design. Because so many people had avoided using compliance, it created a backlog and the compliance team was actually overwhelmed. I asked my team to step in and help track down and document unreviewed materials, and we proactively created alignments between our departments. Instead of compliance being an obstacle, they became an invaluable resource and business partner for marketing. The impact was significant, and over time, the culture of hostility towards compliance dissipated.

I've never understood those who resist necessary business processes. My aim is to identify how processes can be aligned. Being that connector and fostering cross-departmental trust builds strong resources for yourself because people recognize your efforts to add value for everyone. As you undertake this, document everything and build an archive of the knowledge you're creating. Solidify that knowledge and ensure people have access to it so that the processes, relationships, and intellectual capital you develop can be passed on and endure, adding value and building annuities over time.

As you're playing this corporate game and you're leveling up, at some point, you'll encounter challenges akin to reaching a tower. You're on an epic quest of pursuing and obtaining goals such as promotions, salary increases, and enhanced visibility. This journey requires dedication and follow-through, and some people struggle because the process feels exclusive or unobtainable. Many harbor mistrust towards the promotion process within organizations, a sentiment often justified in toxic cultures characterized by favoritism, nepotism, and the overlook of capable internal people because they feel like they're going to get the unicorn from outside. There are a lot of shadow things that can happen in that promotional process, but I do really believe that good people get promoted for good reasons. I believe that good people get promoted because they make a commitment and follow through, and people realize that they are truly dependable. They have good vision, and people can see that there's somebody they can trust, someone who presents the accountability and responsibility of a leader.

I once shared an IG reel telling people to *"Stop Working So Hard"* if they wanted to be a leader. It really upset a lot of people. They defended their hard work and long hours and suggested I meant that leadership was easy. That wasn't the message at all. The real message is that you can be the most technically proficient person in the world, and you can work and code 16 hours a day, and that is simply not going to make you a leader. Instead, take some of that time that you're spending being so dedicated to your technical skill and your technical practice, and redirect it towards spending time to develop yourself as a leader. Many people believe the key to winning the corporate game is overwork and workaholism, but that is actually more of a trauma response and will only end up burning you out. If you really want to be a leader, you need to take time to connect with people, to understand the entirety of the business, and expand yourself beyond just the technical skill set. That's why this concept of working so hard isn't what's going to get you promoted or what's going to level you up in the corporate world. Most likely, it will just get you more technical work. Having a strong work ethic is absolutely critical. If you don't have integrity and a strong work ethic, you might as well not show up. But it's having that extra layer of accountability and responsibility, combined with leadership vision and mindset, that will propel you up that corporate hierarchy.

So, what happens when the tower falls?

What happens when you reach the top and realize, *Oh no, this isn't really where I want to be!* Or perhaps something changes organizationally, and you find yourself having to start over. There are a lot of things that can occur, and that's sort of a game reset. There have been times when I've taken steps back so that I could propel myself forward. I've never regretted that, ever. My career path hasn't always been linear, which has been incredibly beneficial for me. This approach allows me to detach from specific outcomes and remain fully engaged in the journey. Being present in what I'm experiencing and learning and understanding how I can apply that knowledge makes me even more productive, creative, and visionary in my next endeavor, whether I'm bringing value to another organization or pursuing my own entrepreneurial projects. A game reset is essentially about leveraging all the knowledge you've accumulated, integrating it, and using it to advance even further.

Action Items and Journal Prompts: Chapter 5

Reflections

- Do you feel like you have different personas for work and home?

- How do you want to be perceived in the workplace? Do you feel like you are seen in the ways you want to be perceived? Examine areas that feel misaligned.

- Are there certain types of personas that trigger you? How do you feel or react to these individuals? In hindsight, would you react differently?

- How attached are you to outcomes, on a scale of 1 (Not At All Attached) to 10 (Absolutely Must Happen)? How does your level of attachment affect your experience?

- When you set a goal for yourself, how likely are you to accomplish it? What helps or hinders you the most?

Actions

- **Play Real Games At Work.** Start a lunchtime tabletop game event. Every Friday, once a month, or any appropriate time, show up with games and invite others to do the same. Get to know each other by playing together. Leaders, I strongly urge you to champion this and participate. You will learn a lot too.

- **Discover Your Archetype.** Take the Corporate Persona Archetype Quiz to learn more about how you express yourself in corporate spaces. https://tapasinnovation.involve.me/corporate-persona-archetype

CHAPTER 6

ALLIANCES AND ADVERSARIES

"Great things in business are never done by one person;
they're done by a team of people."
– Steve Jobs, Businessman, Inventor, and Co-founder of Apple, Inc.

In the corporate world, you will encounter alliances and, unfortunately, sometimes individuals who feel like adversaries and may indeed be so. Some alliances are easy to identify and connect with, while others may be more elusive. That's okay. They may not be accustomed to people who seek to build genuinely productive relationships without an agenda. Look for opportunities to build goodwill within your team and across departments to create alliances. Also, seek ways to initiate these kinds of connections among others. In a healthy corporate culture, all departments work towards the same purpose, with collaboration and open lines of communication encouraged and supported.

Toxic cultures, on the other hand, tend to promote adversarial behaviors that leave individuals feeling fearful or threatened, leading to more conflict. There's a sense that colleagues are working against you and each other. As trust and a sense of security diminish, defense mechanisms kick in, escalating conflict into emotional reactivity. In such environments, people become territorial and secretive, guarding information and authority as if they were currency. When companies foster an intense culture of competition, it may yield short-term financial gain, but over time, the culture will deteriorate, making it difficult to retain talented individuals due to emotional burnout. A common response to a highly competitive culture is the creation of silos to protect and maintain control. Silos often develop their own microcultures, which could be more or less toxic than the overarching organizational culture. Regardless, they are problematic because they promote further division and disconnection within the organization.

My approach is rooted in the concept that we're all on the same team when working in an organization, and the purpose and goals should be shared. Ideally, everyone is aligned with the organization's purpose and values, and all employees understand their role and its direct impact on that purpose. When everyone works towards a shared purpose, with a clear understanding of their contribution to that goal, productivity and morale increase organically. It's important to recognize that creating a shared purpose and vision must take precedence over creating tiny kingdoms that ultimately drain energy and resources rather than contributing to the organizational goals.

One way to move in this direction is to stop tolerating tyranny as a means of leadership. Individuals who pit their employees against each other, believing it maximizes productivity, are relying on outdated practices and, in reality, diminishing productivity. Instead, we need to recognize and reward collaboration, acknowledging that when we collaborate, we promote shared successes. Elevating the value of this approach is essential, not just in practice but also in terms of long-term ROI. This doesn't mean we ignore the individual contributions made by team members. Celebrating individual achievements is important, but it should be connected to the idea of contribution and that we are all moving things forward towards a common goal.

When I played softball, I played first base, and I felt just as thrilled when my pitcher struck someone out as I did when I caught the ball for an out at first. Who made the play didn't matter; what mattered was that we were working together as a synchronized team with immense trust and respect for each other. This allowed us to play off of each other's strengths. Applying this concept to business functions helps break down silos and build trust. As a team player, there was never any doubt about how my role, or anyone else's, contributed to our goal of winning the game. Yes, we were competing against another team – competition itself isn't inherently negative – but we never competed against each other. If we had, we wouldn't have been successful, which we were.

In corporate culture, a great place to begin is by creating leadership alignment across departments. I've never been part of an organization without departmental dependencies. Leaders have a tremendous opportunity to foster team connectedness by identifying and establishing these alignments, where processes might overlap, instead of looking at it from the perspective of competition or territory. Seeing a dependency from a perspective of identifying shared pain or potential opportunity and then collaborating on those solutions creates powerful shifts in organizational energy. When we acknowledge cross-departmental dependencies and recognize the need for shared resources, we find opportunities to streamline processes and make resources more effective or more impactful within the organization. This requires communication. We have to talk to each other. We need to take the time to talk and recognize that there's productivity in those conversations and in those connections.

Once people trust each other enough to see each other as allies – or even better, united by a shared purpose – then identifying and celebrating those shared wins will improve the culture exponentially.

One thing I've been taught, almost as a mantra, is the concept that process quells emotion. There's a bit of truth to that. I don't believe we'll ever fully remove emotion from the corporate world as we might wish or think we should, and frankly, I'm not sure it's beneficial to even try. But I do think that there's value in recognizing that not everything in business needs to be emotional. Emotions often come into play when there are breakdowns in systems that create pressure and stress. Depending on the company, this may be by design or accident. Most people don't feel confident or safe enough to speak up without fear of being vilified or labeled as troublemakers. Companies and leaders need to be more receptive to frontline feedback. Many stressors can be resolved through changing or refining processes to address pain points. Process development should align needs and actions. So when discussing cross-departmental processes or those impacting multiple teams, this development shouldn't occur in isolation. Everyone affected should have a way to contribute insight. While leaders hold responsibility for decision-making, I strongly advocate for democratic collaboration and the importance of hearing diverse perspectives to fully understand the impact of any actions or processes implemented.

Another issue that has become mission-critical in our society is generational warfare. We're disconnected generationally, which harms us both in business and socially. So, I'm just going to say it: stop blaming other generations. Seriously, everyone, just stop. This is especially true for older generations who criticize younger ones. It's illogical to criticize a group of people you've played a role in shaping. If you're unhappy with what you observe in younger generations, the first step is to look inward. Here are some facts everyone needs to accept: First, millennials are now adults – fully grown, in their 40s, paying taxes, and raising families, though they may struggle with homeownership through no fault of their own. Millennials are no longer twenty. They are not the ones who asked for the participation trophies. Their parents are the ones who gave them to them. We need to recognize that, as a generation, Millennials are the new leaders in our workforce. And here's a revelation for some: Gen Z has entered the workforce. That's right, Gen Z is applying for and landing jobs, and they're bringing fresh and interesting contributions to the workforce. A recent LinkedIn study showed that 87% of Gen Z employees would leave a job if it did not align with their values.[51] Leaders need to consider that fact when they think about this very talented group who, like all generations, can be a little misunderstood. And that's okay, to a degree.

I'm a proud Gen Xer, and one belief I hold about my generation is that we should be tapped more for our resilience and creativity. It's a core and defining trait of our generation. I understand it's weird to make sweeping statements about generations because, in reality, we all have our unique experiences and will show up as who we are. Unfortunately, these sweeping generalizations often turn into stereotypes, leading to bias. This brings me to my next point, which I know is going to piss off a lot of people who are caught up in the generational warfare going up and down. The Baby Boomer generation is often perceived as blaming others, yet they also face a lot of criticism. My feeling is that this cycle of blame only serves to deepen our divisions rather than allowing us to learn from one another. We have much to offer each other, and wisdom can emerge from all perspectives. I believe we can find value alignments across generations and view each other more generously. Interestingly, "generous" and "generation" share the same root word, "genus," suggesting a natural alignment.

I firmly believe there are universal values we can all agree on, or at least we can create spaces to explore and remain open-minded about understanding each other's experiences. Part of this involves changing our views on what it means to belong to a certain generation. Reducing media influence and seeking real-life experiences with people from different

---

[51] INOP, "Gen Z Workforce: Values as the Catalyst for Job Change." *LinkedIn*, 1 June 2023, www.linkedin.com/pulse/gen-z-workforce-values-catalyst-job-change-inop-ai/.

generations is a great starting point. One practice I've adopted is networking with people younger than me. I strive to understand their mindset, experiences, and what drives and motivates them. I'm often more than impressed by their ambition and vision – I'm truly inspired. It gives me hope. Then, I go to environments where I hear people complaining about how problematic other generations are, describing work styles and habits that they find immensely frustrating. My response is always the same: that hasn't been my experience. Whether someone is older, younger, or the same age as me, I nearly always find something valuable to learn from them.

I'm also tired of hearing claims that people don't want to work. That's bullshit. People do want to work and work hard. They just want to be valued and respected within their work environments. This holds true for people of all ages. Everyone wants to contribute meaningfully, and it's our responsibility to enable them to do so. We need to make working environments sustainable and a place where people can thrive, regardless of what generation they're from.

Action Items and Journal Prompts: Chapter 6

Reflections

- Do you feel like you are a part of a unified culture in your workplace? Describe what works and what could be improved.

- How do you relate to your co-workers? What makes you see someone as an ally or an adversary? Are you ever adversarial?

- Are you aware of generational bias in your workplace or yourself? Consider how these biases impede the ability to motivate or inspire others.

- Bosses, approach your team with a spirit of respect and curiosity. What can you learn from each other? What can you learn about yourself? Examine this by journaling.

- Employees, ask your boss a question about their experience and actively listen to their response. What assumptions are you making about them? Did you learn anything new? Journal your thoughts.

Actions

- **Ignore the Silos.** How much do you understand other departments outside your own and their challenges? Make a list outlining how you view each department in your environment, including your assumptions, both positive and negative. Introduce yourself to people and ask them about their work. Review your assumptions and update your perspective as you learn more.

- **Generation Free.** Identify an activity that you associate with a specific generation – something people older or younger than you do. It's your perspective, so you decide what it is. Then, experience it joyfully and completely. Try something that you judge generationally in this way with a curious mind. What is there for you to learn?

CHAPTER 7

THE BOSS EFFECT

"In the past, a leader was a boss. Today's leaders must be partners with their people... they no longer can lead solely based on positional power."
– Ken Blanchard, Author, Business Consultant, and Motivational Speaker

If you've had a job, then you've had a boss. Even if you were a boss, unless you owned the company you worked for, you still had a boss. Essentially, everyone has had this experience. Maybe not everyone has been a boss, but most people in the corporate world have had the experience of having to report to one. Your boss can positively impact you by helping you elevate, expand, and learn so you rise in your career, or they can have the opposite effect, hindering your growth for a variety of reasons. Additionally, your boss significantly affects your health. As mentioned earlier, bosses have an enormous effect on the employee's day-to-day life. Often, the way employees end and start their day is shaped by their relationship with their boss. I've known many people who become physically ill on Sunday night, dreading the depleting, energetic experience awaiting them at work the next day.

If a boss isn't serving their employees or is present for reasons other than to get the job done, it's a problem for both employees and the business. A boss's role is to guide and motivate, taking responsibility for their employees' productivity. If they fail to serve effectively, they can cause significant harm, not only on an individual level but also to teams as a whole. The damage is real and extends beyond the workplace, impacting mental and physical health and personal relationships – essentially, all aspects of a person's life. At some point, we might even ask ourselves: do we even really need bosses? If there is the potential for a boss to have so much impact on your life, and you have unskilled, untrained bosses who are managing people poorly – bosses who are creating more stressors, not removing obstacles to promote productivity – then what is the net positive result of that?

Part of the problem is the amount of control and authority given to individuals based on their titles. Your boss has the power to hire and fire you and can significantly influence your life and career. If you win the lottery and get a great boss, the impact can last a lifetime. Most people experience a series of unskilled bosses. However, a lack of training doesn't automatically make someone a "bad boss." I believe everyone tries to do their best with what they know. Some people just have more awareness and knowledge than others. It is up to the organization to set a standard for leadership and management and then make sure that resources and training are available and implemented.

Managers and Leaders

Are you a manager, or are you a leader? From my perspective, managers should be managing things, not people. Project managers manage projects, time, money, and resources. I think the notion that people are resources feels very dehumanizing, yet it's a reality in the corporate world. It's fair to acknowledge that people are often viewed as resources. In terms of management, it should only occur from a strategic, high-level perspective: What resources are needed to complete the job? What skills are required, and what do those skills cost? However, actively managing and controlling people's actions is a system bound for failure, an unwinnable game. Our concept of a boss should lean more towards that of a coach or mentor. While managers should be managing things, bosses should be leading people and be held to higher standards.

They should focus on elevating others, not merely delegating tasks, which brings us to the leadership mindset. The real distinction between being a leader and merely a boss or manager is that leadership involves setting and exemplifying standards of behavior to uplift everyone and everything around them. Ideally, leaders demonstrate self-discipline and emotional intelligence, capable of being visionary while also being attentive to details. Leadership encompasses a broad skill set that includes intuition, logic, confidence, authority, and empathy. The best leaders are those who can integrate these aspects effectively.

However, there are some unfortunate Boss Personas you might encounter or be familiar with. I wanted to examine these personas to increase our awareness of what might drive their energy and how we can navigate these situations. I refer to this kind of thing as "when your boss isn't a boss," referring to individuals who fall short of the boss or leadership title.

The Inexperienced Boss

Firstly, many bosses are inexperienced, but they aren't inherently bad people. In fact, they likely have a genuine desire to succeed and impress both their team and superiors. The extent of their effectiveness largely depends on their preparedness for the role. Inexperience can lead to common issues, such as micromanagement, primarily stemming from a lack of confidence and experience. Without sufficient experience to learn, they may struggle to trust the process and maybe even other people. They also haven't been able to develop their confidence, so it's important for them to be hyper-involved in everything that everybody's doing because they don't ever want to be caught in a situation where they don't know what's going on.

"Inexperienced Bosses" often experience a degree of imposter syndrome in their new roles. Consequently, they may fail to set sufficient boundaries. It's not uncommon for "Inexperienced Bosses" or new managers to want to be friends with their employees, aiming to foster a relatable culture. However, in doing so, they risk sacrificing their authority. They may become overly personal, show favoritism, or find themselves easily triggered by diverse personalities. They haven't had enough experience to know themselves well enough to understand how to be responsive to these different types of personalities that they're responsible for guiding and leading. They tend to struggle with expressing authority in healthy ways, if at all, and may not be able to delegate, either hoarding all the work or just dumping it off on somebody.

The thing about the "Inexperienced Boss" is that they have a lot of potential if they're properly supported. I mean, we all have to start somewhere. If we're aware that these are some of the obstacles or potential pitfalls of that "Inexperienced Boss" right out of the gate, we can be working on that awareness. For example, instead of micromanaging, how can I build trust within our team and still maintain authority?

The I Don't Wanna Be a Boss

Another "Boss" persona I've encountered frequently, and for whom I have much empathy, is the "I Don't Wanna Be a Boss." Often, this individual is a highly skilled SME (subject matter expert) who, to increase compensation or advance their career, finds themselves in a managerial role with no alternative path for growth or development. While they may make exceptional technical mentors, they often lack the soft skills to truly excel in the other aspects of management and leadership. The struggle is real for these individuals; while not every aspect of a job needs to be fun, the stress they experience can be significant.

They usually don't have real experience in managing and have spent most of their life developing their technical skills. They've just gotten so good at what they do that they are in some ways irreplaceable, and their organization wants to retain them. This is just really the only path that makes sense economically. The "I Don't Wanna be a Boss" tends to stay very hands-on with the work because that's where their passion lies and where they feel the most comfortable. They don't have any interest in the administrative aspect of managing. They're probably not going to be tracking time sheets very well, or if they do, it will be in an overly analytical way. They're going to try to operate in the space where they're still more focused on the work they enjoy doing, and they will tend to take production roles in projects as opposed to delegating. I know that some businesses are starting to recognize this issue.

Often, what happens is that an individual gets promoted to a managerial position and then doesn't stay very long because they become miserable and disconnected from the work they're truly passionate about, leading them to eventually move on anyway. Some businesses are starting to recognize the cost of that loss, and they are creating SME advancement tracks alongside leadership advancement tracks that are equally valued. I am a big believer in doing this. In some situations, it could be very beneficial to have co-leadership, where there is an SME that serves in a technical mentor capacity working collaboratively with a soft skills leader. These two act as a functional team, and they lead with authority together. These are things that we should look at in terms of what we can change. We can improve situations like this and create opportunities for people without making them miserable.

The Absent Boss

The next boss that everybody loves is the "Absent Boss." In my experience, this person doesn't really want to be a boss for any reason other than status. I think that self-motivated workers tend to actually love these bosses because they appreciate this management style. "Absent Bosses" are not micromanagers; they're usually not even available, and some workers like this until there's a crisis. That's when they need their boss to show up, and they're not there. Frequently, the "Absent Boss" is already on the way to the next thing because this is a status move. As they gain more status, they're immediately looking for that next opportunity to move up. They're disengaged and undependable to the people they are supposed to lead, but may be very connected to the higher echelon leaders. They're not focused on building team culture. They might not even be aware of team culture.

Another version of this persona to consider is that it's highly possible the "Absent Boss" may be moving towards the end of their career, or transitioning away from the career they've been in towards something else. They may be looking towards future transitions and are just disengaged. They may also have significant changes happening in their personal lives that pull them away from work life. In this situation, there may be more overall empathy for their unique situation, but the team will still be impacted in negative ways.

The Bully Boss

The "Bully Boss" is really the most stereotyped boss, and the one that causes the most damage to corporate culture as a whole and to individuals personally. They are often described as narcissistic. They are emotionally reactive and typically quick to express anger. They may do demeaning things with their staff, such as belittling or calling people out in front of others, creating an intimidating environment. They often thrive in a culture of intimidation and fear. It's frustrating because, in a lot of ways, the "Bully Boss" is celebrated in our culture. You see it portrayed in movies and media as a domineering force of power, slamming their fist on the table, belting out orders, and demanding that things happen, primarily instilling fear. It unquestionably gets things done, but at a huge expense. For a long time, we have ignored or maybe not even seen the cost. But "Bully Bosses" are responsible for causing a lot of physical and emotional damage to workers' health and, frankly, to the health of their own businesses.

"Bully Bosses" are tolerated for the short-term gains they make possible. It does seem, however, that they're being tolerated less and less. People are starting to recognize that there really is a cost; this cost outweighs any potential benefits of this type of behavior.

The "Not Your Boss"

This leads me to my favorite boss, who is *not* my favorite boss, which is "Not Your Boss." They may be a peer to your boss. They might be your boss's boss. Whoever they are, you don't directly report to them, but this person tends to disrespect boundaries, and they like to flaunt authority. They aren't going to respect the proper processes that are in place to get work done. They're not going to be collaborative or supportive. This person will come to you with a totally unreasonable demand where they've created an emergency that doesn't need to be an emergency. A lot of times, this person may even try to undermine your actual boss, as they may have an agenda with nefarious intentions.

They're difficult to work with because they are usually executives or bosses, and they are just flaunting authority. Depending on the culture or the environment, an employee may not feel very empowered to speak up, set boundaries, or to even try to negate that kind of energy. What's worse, if they are undermining your boss, your boss isn't going to be able to do anything for you either because they've already given up that authority to this individual. This means that Not Your Boss creates a lot of challenges in corporate spaces because, functionally, they aren't team players.

The Best Boss

I would like to finish by talking about the best boss. The "Best Boss" is not one specific persona type. I believe all types of people can become great bosses with their unique styles and expressions. However, there are specific traits that align with a true leadership mindset. A visionary boss willing to grow personally demonstrates this. No boss is perfect; mistakes are inevitable. What distinguishes the best bosses – or "enlightened executives" as I call them – is their self-awareness and willingness to learn from anyone and any situation.

Their awareness allows them to lead with both authority and empathy, understanding that it's possible to hold a space of authority and still care about the people that you have to direct or guide. I think that a really good leadership boss is showing up for you as a coach, mentor, and role model. They celebrate your success. They don't use failures as a way to demoralize or diminish people but rather as an opportunity to teach. They appreciate and understand the value of the team and what it means for the team to be connected, to trust each other, and to be able to depend on each other.

They also see the importance of nurturing individual talents and allowing each person their moment in the spotlight. There's a need for companies to invest in training people to be effective bosses. It involves helping people learn how to be more connected with themselves, how to be more emotionally aware, and how to become more intuitive so that they can really truly show up and be an integrated leader who is making decisions from a higher space of purpose instead of working just strictly from their ego or from a place of fear.

Action Items and Journal Prompts: Chapter 7

Reflections

- How do you define leadership? Do you see yourself as a leader? Write about how that looks for you.

- Have you ever had a "Bad Boss"? Think about the worst one and write down what made them so bad. List the qualities. What did you learn about yourself while working for them? Now, do the same thing for your "Best Boss."

- Reflect on a time when you worked for someone who lacked leadership experience, but was still a good person. How did you respond or react to them? Were you able to see them objectively or feel empathy?

- Where has a boss had the most influence on you? Was it positive or negative? What would you do differently?

- When do you feel a sense of authority? How do you express it?

Actions

- **Put It In Writing.** Write a letter to one of your past bosses, explaining to them how they impacted your life. You don't have to send it, but if the impact was positive or significant, it is worth it to consider how they would feel knowing that. If you think the result would be beneficial, then send the letter.

- **Build Your Best Boss Playlist.** Do you have a favorite "Best Boss Song" – something that builds you energy and confidence and makes you feel great? If you don't, find one. If you do, remember to play it when you need it. Better yet, make a whole playlist and share it with your team.

CHAPTER 8

THERE'S NO CRYING IN BOARDROOMS

"Tenderness and kindness are not signs of weakness and despair,
but manifestations of strength and resolution."
– Kahlil Gibran, Lebanese-American Writer, Power, and Visual Artist

Anybody who's played sports knows that there's no crying in baseball, right? Many of us were taught that to be a real athlete and to be an effective sportsman: we had to be tough, we had to be strong. It might hurt, and you might get hurt, but you have to push through that pain and let that pain make you stronger. It's a powerful way of thinking and conditioning. It's a way to approach environments where lives are at risk, or aggressive competition is the only point. But I surmise that we've taken this approach, which works in a highly competitive space or in a space where survival is the critical consideration, and adopted it as the ideal model for corporate leadership. It's also universally understood that there's no crying in boardrooms either. When we think of an athlete, soldier, or a first responder, we tend to think of their responses as highly reactive. They seem to just jump into action and act without thinking. This isn't reactive behavior, though. It is highly responsive. Extensive training and conditioning create the responsiveness that allows muscle memory and instincts to take over and for emotions to be appropriately compartmentalized. But those emotions still need to be processed, and culturally, we're not doing so well on that front.

Whenever I think about the structure and order we have crafted into business, I think about sacred geometry. Why would I associate this with the energy that happens in corporate spaces? In sacred geometry, shapes are believed to have specific properties. The two shapes that I want to talk about are cubes and spheres. It fits in well with our boardroom and baseball theme. Boardrooms are essentially large cubes, and with baseballs, we're throwing around a bunch of spheres. What do cubes represent? Cubes represent and symbolize structure and mobility. In essence, they are containers of information and knowledge. When I first learned that, and I started thinking about the levels of cubes that exist in the corporate environment, it made perfect sense. We have these large buildings that are essentially giant cubes, and our large buildings are broken down into offices that are sub-cubes, and then we have what we literally call "cubicles," which are just even smaller cubes. Then we have filing cabinets, boxes, and containers to hold all this knowledge and information, so smaller cubes. Then we get our computers, and for the longest time, computers effectively looked like cubes, and they still function that way symbolically. Even when we think about spreadsheets, they are just boxes, yet they're so complex, and they hold so much data that they act and perform like a cube. It makes sense that in the world of business, the cube would be sort of the essence of the structure that business and corporate strategy would run on because it's a very logic-driven and information-based enterprise. We have to have a way to contain all of this logic and information, and cubes just make that seem easy.

Which brings me to the sphere. What makes the sphere so incredibly powerful is that it's the simplest shape. It's simple, but the sphere is the one shape that can contain every other shape. The sphere represents wholeness and completeness. When I think about physics in the context of cubes, I think about how we have really subdivided ourselves and have created these subdivisions of departments that are very necessary for order and structure. We understand that, higher up, we have subdivisions of hierarchy, but we as individuals are also expected to compartmentalize and subdivide ourselves.

We're asked to bring just our cube to work – just the logical piece of who we are – and to leave everything else aside. We are taught that all those other elements and energies are distractions. This mindset, I believe, has fostered a highly reactive culture.

It has allowed a system of emotional immaturity to develop, leading to a preference for managing things, analyzing data, and viewing individuals as mere assets. Emotional maturity has been sidelined in leadership roles. Numerous studies highlight the stress present in business, and companies have responded by implementing wellness programs, offering free gym memberships, and providing mental health care. While these initiatives are helpful, they don't address the core issue if the culture and environment continue to undermine individuals' energy.

When considering the concept of cubes and spheres, embracing the entirety of business and the individuals working within it would be far more beneficial. Imagine if we could show up as spheres fully containing everything within us, including that cube space of intellect and knowledge, but also bringing in heart-centered energy and other sorts of tools, like intuition and empathy, that have been negated because they can't be easily measured in terms of transactional value. They can't be placed into a cube, thereby creating a limitation.

In the context of the boardroom, when we consider the expectations of what is supposed to be happening there, we think about leadership. The boardroom is a symbol of status: the place where the masterminds come together and strategize. These are the visionaries; they're the people running the company. You imagine this environment of people coming together in these boardroom spaces, making big decisions, and working through serious problems. It's what we want to believe is happening, and we want to believe it is happening for great reasons.

Yet, behaviors in boardrooms vary widely, from productive and innovative to negative and even abusive, including sexism, racism, and hostility. The C-suite, representing the highest-level executives, often experiences a significant disconnect, not just with the organization but also in understanding their roles' responsibility and accountability. This disconnection, whether by design or not, prevents us from achieving wholeness and from being fully integrated spheres in the business world.

What if, instead of the C-suite, we had a "See Sweet"? Imagine having a visionary group fully aligned with both themselves and the company vision. And by "sweet," I mean not in a soft sense, but in the sense of pure magnificence. It would be incredible to have a C-suite aligned in vision and values, where you knew these people united for the organization's greater good. The "See Sweet" would establish real accountability systems tied directly to value alignment and activation, as they should lead and model the organization's value system. They would connect managers and leaders at every level to the company's purpose.

This is how chief executive officers truly live up to their role's title, and there should be an expectation for them to do so. Much of what is required and expected of chief executive officers in businesses often gets delegated to what I refer to as "the culture club." In Corporate America, the culture club isn't a single group or individual; it typically comprises departments that contribute to or take responsibility for managing and nurturing the organization's culture. I consider HR, sales, technology, and marketing as central to addressing business problems that are often created by leadership and can only be solved at that level. An example is high employee turnover due to poor culture, with the expectation placed on HR to recruit more aggressively and develop better retention programs. However, what needs to be resolved are the underlying cultural issues and leadership challenges.

Another example of this is trying to market your way out of a business problem. But as we noted earlier, that's become harder and harder with social media and social transparency. Companies used to be able to hide behind their brands, and if something terrible happened, they could simply rebrand, and they would – like BP. People will forget what the old brand did and the new gets to keep doing the same thing, but with a whole fresh look. It's like putting on a new mask or disguise. Unfortunately, our attention spans are so short that often this still works, but it is becoming more difficult.

Sales and technology also influence how culture gets managed. For sales teams, they often act as a buffer between their customers and any internal cultural issues. While motivated and compensated to move products and sell company services, when internal breakdowns impede their customer relationships, it can create a stressful environment as they strive to appease clients amidst chaos. Technology might not seem directly connected to company culture, but it plays a significant role. Technology systems enable companies to function and interact in various ways. The innovation and flexibility technology brings to organizations add significant value and impact culture. Having worked in technology and organizations with large internal tech groups, I've seen its substantial influence on organizational culture. If technology groups are managed in isolation or are toxic, it can cause issues for other departments reliant on their support, highlighting why technology is integral to the culture club.

Another aspect I believe is crucial for a more holistic business experience is reevaluating HR's roles and responsibilities in alignment with individual and organizational needs. HR should focus more on regulatory and compliance responsibilities, developing benefits and compensation packages, and ensuring proper organizational structure management. However, areas like employee development and advancement, talent and recruiting, and objective employee advocacy could benefit from a dedicated department. This clarity would benefit those working in these environments. Many HR leaders

I've worked with, from middle to senior management, seek advice due to the conflict between their values and the pressures of their HR role. There are highly conflicting requirements. On the one hand, a person has to be the shining, welcoming face of an organization that is pitching and selling the culture, going to job fairs and being present in that way. The same exact person has to lay off an entire group of people when times are bad. That's a very difficult role to put people in, and I don't think that people ultimately function well that way.

I believe human resources should be divided into corporate resources and employee services. Under corporate resources, asset management would include individuals since, in Corporate America, bottom lines and profitability matter. Companies need to sustain earnings to pay their staff, highlighting the realities of corporate operations. However, much of the toxicity in Corporate America stems from failing to recognize the demands placed on individuals to go above and beyond without meeting their needs, all for the sake of profit or a purpose they may not connect with.

This all ties back to leadership aligning with values. I respect organizations that clearly state profit is their bottom line value and manage accordingly. This transparency allows workers to decide their level of emotional, physical, or energetic investment in the job, mirroring the organization's investment in its employees. Investing more in employees typically results in greater returns. A healthier workforce naturally fosters a sustainable, long-lasting environment.

One other thing to consider is whether customers are on board. If the customers are crying out, your organization is obviously in trouble. Customer experience has become both a buzzword and a fresh perspective on customer strategy. Despite years of measuring consumer satisfaction through various methods, "review fatigue" is real. The pressure to respond to follow-up reviews after every interaction can be overwhelming. While some complete reviews to support the individuals they interact with, knowing organizations use these for employee evaluation, the resulting customer data may not accurately reflect the actual experience. Customers increasingly expect companies to actively uphold values, with more than 75% of customers wanting company values to be active for the organizations that they spend money with and the goods that they spend their money on. They care more than companies have typically believed. Consumers also want to do business with companies whose values align with their own, so they are really focusing on that and making decisions on this basis. In a single industry, one retail business might align towards one political side, and another retail business will align towards another political side, and people will actively make choices to spend their money based on their own personal political beliefs and what they want to support. This is already happening, and people are going to continue to make spending decisions in this way. This is just one example of how people are using their values to navigate brand loyalty.

Companies need to recognize the big picture of what's happening, slow down, and maybe take a step back in order to retool. I'm not a strong believer in rebranding. I think rebranding should occur strategically only when there's a legitimate need, such as during a business merger or if a business is genuinely shifting directions. Updating a brand's design to keep it current is one thing, but rebranding to mask bad behavior or the darker aspects of an organization's image is a practice I hope fades away. Companies should instead focus on "*brand rehabilitation,*" delving into their brand to strengthen it from within. This means reinforcing the foundation of the existing brand and truly embracing brand advocacy. If done effectively, you can even leverage crowd-sourced sales through reviews and referrals. A thriving, authentic brand will turn customers into the best advocates. They will feel a deep connection to the brand beyond just transactions. The strongest advocacy comes from a brand alignment that extends from top leadership, through the company's culture and employees, and reaches out to consumers and their networks.

Action Items and Journal Prompts: Chapter 8

Reflections

- Do you think of yourself as more logical or more emotional? In what way are you more comfortable expressing yourself?

- When do you feel the most reactive at work? Are there times you wish you could go back and redo or say something in another way? Write about one of those times and what you would do differently.

- Does your company have a "customer experience" focus? What about the employee experience? How does it affect the overall culture?

- Have you ever witnessed an emotionally triggering situation in the workplace? Did you feel reactive or responsive? How did you feel about how the situation was handled?

- Do you feel safe expressing yourself in your company? If the answer is no, how long can you tolerate feeling that way?

Actions

- **Know Your Support Options.** What resources do you have for mental health support in your company? Do the research and make sure you are taking advantage of available benefits. If your job doesn't provide this type of support, look within your community. Be proactive about mental health care.

- **Take a BREAK.** Take time to establish simple mental health breaks at work. Set 5-min "stretch breaks" to remind yourself to move. Take breaks that are given to you and use them with the intention of self-care. Take time to eat. Take a short walk. Do a quick breathing exercise. Find something consistent that you can do to honor yourself. Model this behavior for others.

Hot Tip for Leaders: Support employee breaks and also *take them yourself!*

CHAPTER 9

BOARD OVERLORDS?

"Customers will never love a company until the employees love it first."
– Simon Sinek, Author of *Start with Why*

I've posed a question to many people and received varied responses: How accountable is the board to the value system of the organization? This question is especially pertinent for public companies with shareholders or boards that operate from an investor perspective. Can boards embody and uphold values, and should they? In many cases, they serve as the overlords for organizational culture. Essentially, a board's role is to ensure the organization functions in a way that benefits shareholders, prioritizing the company's profitability and long-term growth. But does this alignment always occur? Customers seek value alignment and transparency, wanting assurance that it extends through every level of the organization. Boards sometimes appear as shadowy figures in the background, often unknown or unrecognized, yet they wield significant influence and control over organizational decisions.

Mergers can often kill culture, especially when organizations finally come together. When that happens, it can cost billions of dollars and result in complete failure. In the context of what boards are accountable for and the expectations they face, it's important to consider that one of the reasons these mergers fail is because the cultures aren't aligned, and in many cases, alignment is not a possibility. We can look at the Time Warner/AOL failed merger, resulting in hostility and a historic $99B+ net loss as a blatant example of this type of failure.[52] According to the Harvard *Business Review*, multiple studies put the "fail rate" of corporate mergers somewhere between 70% and 90%, which seems both astronomical and also wasteful.[53] There is a deeply transactional detachment within the M&A process that is able to compartmentalize the people who are directly impacted by these business decisions. Leaders, executives, and board members who are guiding these strategies should have more accountability for the real-life ramifications of their poor decision-making and failed execution of strategy.

Where I am most challenged by all of this is that when they do, the chances of success for everyone increase, so it is baffling to understand why more care and consideration isn't given to this process beyond simply looking at spreadsheets and making assumptions. If boards make decisions strictly based on the bottom line and transactions without taking into account the people involved and their emotions, the mergers are less likely to succeed. Mergers and cultural alignments have a much higher chance of success when these factors are taken into consideration. It seems like simple math.

For example, Boeing merged with McDonnell Douglas in 1997. At that time, they went from being an engineering company to being primarily run by MBAs. This is well-documented. The culture of the company shifted substantially from prioritizing safety and engineering to focusing on the bottom line and profits.

Now, 20 to 25 years later, we can see how this is playing out in real time. Boeing is a huge organization, and culture shifts, especially in large companies, don't happen overnight. It takes time, but for good or bad, when

---

[52] Dumont, Marvin. "4 Biggest Merger and Acquisition Disasters." Investopedia, 21 Feb. 2022, investopedia.com/articles/financial-theory/08/merger-acquisition-disasters.asp.

[53] Kenny, Graham . "Don't Make This Common M&A Mistake." Harvard Business Review, 16 Mar. 2020, hbr.org/2020/03/don't-make-this-common-ma-mistake.

there is a substantial culture shift, it will eventually come through to the consumer. In this case, it comes through in a life-or-death scenario, literally. In 2018 and 2019, a combined total of 346 passengers and crew lost their lives due to mechanical and engineering failures by Boeing.[54] This raises questions about the accountability of the board in upholding these values. Is there accountability in a situation like that, where Boeing's website still says that engineering and safety are their top priorities, but their actions don't match their words? Currently, according to Boeing's own website, they have over 10,000 commercial aircraft in service around the world.[55] There are commercial airlines that only fly Boeing planes. As a consumer, it feels like there is a new report every week of another potential flight calamity – wheels falling off planes, engines catching on fire, gaping holes where doors should be – and I know my confidence in flying has taken a recent nose-dive. Pun intended. Boeing's accountability becomes exponential when considered in totality, but who assumes the responsibility?

Another issue with boardrooms and core company values has to do with egos, particularly the egos in the boardroom and the disparity between the typical worker and high-level executives, whether in the C-suite or higher. The way compensation and bonus packages are designed are not always in alignment with how organizations describe their values, such as valuing their people or the integrity of their values. The disparity between the head of an organization and a worker has grown substantially over just the last generation, the last 20 to 30 years, and it's really unbelievable. The Economic Policy Institute reports that over a roughly 40-year period, and adjusted for

---

[54] Reuters. "Factbox: Boeing's Worst Crashes over the Last Decade." Reuters, 21 Mar. 2022, www.reuters.com/business/aerospace-defense/boeings-worst-crashes-over-last-decade-2022-03-21/.

[55] Boeing. "General Information." www.boeing.com, 2024, www.boeing.com/company/general-info#overview.

inflation, CEO compensation rose 1,460.2%, and in 2021 the compensation ratio of CEO-worker reached an all-time high of 399-1.[56]

And what's worse, even more than the compensation disparity, is when leaders of organizations flat out fail – simply not getting the job done – and still walk away with golden parachutes, receiving excessive compensation for their failure. They also don't seem to experience any real consequences. In the midst of Boeing's ongoing crisis with its 737 MAX, the CEO, president, and board chairman all announced their departures, leaving a company that appears to be in dire straits.[57] A position it seems they were instrumental in attaining for Boeing. It's challenging for the average worker to understand this, especially when they often feel undervalued and unrecognized for their hard work and dedication. Moreover, organizations seem to demand loyalty but are not always willing to reciprocate, creating a sense of disillusionment among workers. We need to closely examine the impact and influence of boards on organizations. There might be opportunities to foster a more positive influence that allows organizations to be profitable while also operating at a higher level of energy and commitment.

A board of directors has the opportunity to influence organizational culture in significant ways, and helping individuals on boards understand the value of a healthy corporate culture is critical.[58] I focus a lot on M&A activity in this chapter because it is so fraught that there is clearly room for improvement. But due to their extraordinary potential to create long-lasting results, any organization with a board should be examining the motivations

---

[56] Bivens, Josh, and Jori Kandra. "CEO Pay Has Skyrocketed 1,460% since 1978: CEOs Were Paid 399 Times as Much as a Typical Worker in 2021." Economic Policy Institute, 4 Oct. 2022, www.epi.org/publication/ceo-pay-in-2021/.

[57] Reeder, Leslie Josephs,Phil LeBeau,Meghan. "Boeing CEO to Step down in Broad Management Shakeup as 737 Max Crisis Weighs on Aerospace Giant." CNBC, 25 Mar. 2024, www.cnbc.com/2024/03/25/boeing-ceo-board-chair-commercial-head-out-737-max-crisis.html.

[58] "Corporate Culture and the Role of Boards." Harvard.edu, 2016, corpgov.law.harvard.edu/2016/08/13/corporate-culture-and-the-role-of-boards/.

and perspectives being projected by its members. Are they exhibiting the integrity and behavior of a thriving and sustainable business? Do they pay attention to the needs of their organization – both employees and customers? And most importantly, does the board completely embody and express the organizational values? These are important questions that I think we need to ask in order to heal and address toxic cycles in business.

Action Items and Journal Prompts: Chapter 9

Reflections

- Do you think shareholders have any ethical or moral responsibility with respect to the health of a company's culture? Consider why or why not.

- As an employee working for an organization with a board of directors, are you aware of their influence within your organization? Does it matter to you, and why or why not?

- Think about your 3 favorite brands. Write about the qualities of each brand that makes them stand out to you. How much influence do you think the board has on your experience with this brand? Explore each brand to learn more.

- If you are a leader within an organization that has a board of directors, how do you feel about your relationship or influence with your board? What are their expectations of you and how does that affect your day-to-day performance and decisions?

Actions

- **Get to know your Board of Directors!** Seriously, who are they and what do they do? Many board members have a wealth of knowledge and experience you can learn about simply by reading and learning about them. It is interesting to gain insight into the people who have such influence in your company.

- **Attend a Board Meeting.** If it is possible, introduce yourself to someone who is on a board and learn more about their role.

CHAPTER 10

BEYOND LOGOS

"Until you make the unconscious conscious, it will direct your life and you will call it fate."
– Carl G. Jung, Swiss Psychiatrist and Psychoanalyst

When I talk about vibrating at a higher energetic level, I know it sounds a little *"woooo."* But I am a corporate mystic, so there's a little *"woooo"* in my message. Ethos is expressed through our morality, ethics, and integrity. Our ethos is what allows people to connect to us or trust us. When we have a strong, aligned ethos, then our integrity isn't in question. Basically, we are who we say we are. Logos and pathos functionally exist as different sides of the same coin. Our logos is our capacity for logic and reason. It's our logical mind, which we might call our "left brain." Our pathos is our emotional sensibility, our emotional energy, what we would call our "right brain." Ideally, there is an alignment between logos and pathos. Logic and emotions would be in alignment, they would function together, and from this alignment, a strong, personal ethos is expressed.

This alignment of logos, pathos, and ethos gives you a deeper understanding of who you are. It helps you to be discerning and aware of your emotional responses, with the ability to make logical decisions. When you can access all of the information around you using your intuition, your senses, and both your emotions and your logic mind, then you are working from your whole higher self. That's a simple explanation of how a strong ethos should function, and that is what emotional intelligence looks like.

In business, we haven't historically valued all of that. We've put an emphasis on the logos and the logic, so much so that we created actual logos that are emblems of our identity. Logos in business are used to communicate quickly. A person should be able to look at a well-designed logo and understand something relevant about what it represents. Regardless of the symbol, it should immediately tie back to the core identity of the organization in a memorable way. Every time you see it, that logo should reinforce what that organization represents, what they're about, who they are, and what their values are. All of that should come through a logo, which is why good logos have been traditionally valuable for an organization. This is one indication of the extent to which logos (the logic mind) has become the foundation on which a business is built and a literal representation of business identity.

Which brings us to pathos. Satya Nadella, CEO of Microsoft, said it best when he was referencing our need for emotional intelligence in an interview.[59] He was talking about soft skills and acknowledged that empathy is arguably the hardest skill to learn. The ability to genuinely empathize with those around us, to feel and express sincere emotion and concern, is challenging in a corporate world that's heavily focused on glorifying logos. Opening up to that level of pathos, or emotions, can seem daunting, and perhaps for good reason.

When we consider words associated with pathos, such as pathology and pathological, they often convey chaos or a lack of control. Yet, within this chaos lies immense value, information, and energy capable of being organized in ways that create limitless possibilities. Ignoring our emotional side creates

[59] Kirschner, Kylie. "Microsoft CEO Satya Nadella Says Empathy Isn't a Soft Skill – It's Actually 'the Hardest Skill We Learn'." *Business Insider*, Sep. 2023, www.businessinsider.com/microsoft-ceo-satya-nadella-empathy-hard-not-soft-skill-2023-10.

a deficit, limiting access to valuable resources. This can lead to leaders adopting fear-based or highly reactive leadership styles due to a lack of inner work and alignment, impacting their ethos. Many leaders focus solely on external issues, neglecting the potential solutions within themselves. Thus, they lead from a place of fear and ignorance rather than a heart-centered space, generating more fear. This creates an environment where people exist in perpetual survival mode. Science shows that living in a constant state of fear harms us on every level – hormonally, physically, emotionally, mentally, and spiritually – making it crucial for Corporate America to acknowledge this. Leadership is evolving to embrace more emotional responsiveness, recognizing the value of navigating various situations beyond mere logic.

When we define ethos for ourselves, it's essential to understand we're discussing our personal values and comprehending our value systems. I view values as mutable, capable of evolving over time. Your values aren't necessarily things you would die for. As individuals, we hold core principles – beliefs that remain unchanged and define who we are fundamentally. These are beliefs we might fight or even die for. However, most of us don't possess many unwavering beliefs since our primary aim is survival. The necessity to defend or sacrifice life for a cause must be of utmost importance. I distinguish these guiding ethics from our value systems, which are more adaptable. Our values, to a large extent, reflect what we're willing to negotiate and invest in. For valid reasons, values are transactional. What we value at twenty can significantly differ from what we value at forty or sixty. By considering our values in terms of spending, their nature becomes clearer. Analyzing where we invest our time, money, energy, and effort reveals our true values. The areas where we engage in a transactional exchange (what we choose to invest in) highlight what we genuinely value.

I challenge people often. I'll ask people what their values are. I'll hear things like, "I value family," "I value my health," or "I value volunteering or doing things for others." Then I start breaking things down, asking them how they're spending their time, money, and energy. Often, the things they said they valued the most get deprioritized because that's not where the spend is happening. For example, they're working a lot without ever taking vacation time or a day off. Even through the weekends, they just keep working. In their mind, they're telling themselves they're working because they're supporting their family, but in many ways, they're spending so much time with their work that they're neglecting their health and their family. It's incongruent, and while it might seem logical, it doesn't feel aligned. I call these kinds of values *aspirational* because until you make the decision to prioritize your stated values with concrete actions, they're going to be in a misalignment. While you say you value it, you're not acting in alignment with your value.

Most of the time, our values come from a variety of sources. We adopt many values before we really understand what our own values are. As we grow up, our family systems have values, our spiritual or church systems have values, our friend systems, social groups, communities – we get values thrown at us from all over the place. Every time we interact with another individual, we're interacting with their values, and we may not value the exact same things. So, there's a negotiation that's happening within us all the time. We have to decide what and how we want to negotiate and what we are unwilling to negotiate. My goal is to help people to think about how they prioritize their own values and see how they can activate the values that they want to prioritize. As you become more attuned to yourself over time, that's how you begin expressing your core ethos: you show up for yourself with your values consistently intact and people begin to clearly understand who you are.

Another important thing to understand about your values is that it's not about other people judging you and your values. There's an old saying that I reflect on often: "What other people think of me is none of my business." It's true. I don't care what your values are for you. I only care about them to the degree that they create a conflict for me. What's important to me is honoring and knowing my own values and recognizing when they are being compromised.

Maybe I've gone too far, perhaps I've over-negotiated, and *I'm being a people-pleaser. I'm not taking care of my own health,* and *I'm putting everybody else's needs first.* In that scenario, I'm not acknowledging my own values. When something like this occurs with consistency, over time, the message becomes *"what I value isn't as important as what other people value,"* and it creates emotional triggers and behavior patterns, such as passive aggression.

Organizational Ethos

Organizational values are a bit different than individual values. To me, they function somewhere between personal values and those principles that are more strongly held. I believe this because, in my view, organizational values should be less mutable and more rigid. They should help define the company's purpose and the company itself. Organizational values should be actionable and easy for employees to understand and express. Leaders should be able to point out exactly how a value is being expressed in their organization or company.

People in companies often complain that company values are just values on paper. It is important for leaders of organizations to listen to this feedback instead of ignoring or denying it. Right now is a great time for companies to stop and examine their values, considering how they are expressed, and if they are more than just logical. If leaders can't clearly define how a value is being expressed, it's important to acknowledge that it's really not a value.

Employees absolutely need to know and understand the ethos of the company they're working for. They're going to find out one way or another, and if it's a toxic environment, they're probably going to find out in really unfortunate ways. When they do find out, they will likely express that toxicity outward by sharing their experiences with others. Unfortunately, some employees will also internalize this toxicity, allowing it to affect their health and diminish their spirit. If the organization is toxic or unhealthy, over time, employees will find ways to empower themselves, and those might not always be ideal solutions.

Organizations are able to empower employees to express themselves on their behalf with a strong, healthy ethos and an active value system. This is not about redesigning logos. This is about changing perspectives. We need to rethink business strategy in terms of workability and health that allows us to thrive – as individuals, in business, and socially – within our community. We've become divided and disconnected, compartmentalized into too many little boxes and labels. While this compartmentalization might feel restrictive, there are a lot of opportunities for businesses to break through the stagnation, build from what works with fresh approaches, and help people step back into purpose. There are ways that we can learn to associate financial value with our ethos values and recognize that there is a return on the investment of values. We can learn to redefine what success looks like in a way that allows everybody to celebrate and participate. None of this has to be diminished or taken from anybody. It can be truly a manifestation of expansion.

Action Items and Journal Prompts: Chapter 10

Reflections

- Reflect on your values and principles. What deeply held beliefs do you carry? How do you express them? Have any changed over time or based on your personal experience?

- Do you notice when you're in survival mode? What do you notice first - actions, thoughts, or feelings? Examine how you respond to these higher-self alerts.

- Think about a value that you are willing to negotiate, such as working extra hours or taking time for yourself. Examine the flexibility of that value and how you feel about it. Do your negotiations align with how you feel? In what ways, or how are they different?

- Do you know your company's core values? Which of them resonates the most with your own?

- How would you describe your company's ethos? Who in your organization seems to embody or express that ethos the most?

Actions

- **Value Your Values**: Give yourself 100 points. Now, make a list of what you value and assign points to your values. Consider how much time, energy, or resources are dedicated to this value. Is it worth 5 points or 50? It's up to you to decide. For the next few days, try to observe your actions - what values are you expressing the most? Are there any on your list that don't show up in your day-to-day life? Make adjustments to your list as needed.

- **Activate Your Values**: Take 3 values you want to prioritize and create a Value Activation Plan. List ways that these values can be actively expressed. For example, an individual might list "I value time with family." and commit to a daily routine that prioritizes spending time with family. A business leader might list "I value innovation." and then create a space for active brainstorming where people feel safe and heard enough to express themselves. The goal is to transform an aspirational value into a measurable action.

CHAPTER 11

CULTURE SHIFT

"There's no magic formula for great company culture. The key is just to treat your staff how you would like to be treated."
– Richard Branson, Founder, Virgin Group

What we really need is a true culture shift in how we approach corporate culture. Earlier, I stated employee turnover can cost an organization with 100 employees up to $2.6 million annually, on average. For a small to mid-sized company, that is an unsustainable loss over time. Employee turnover leads to other costly issues, such as customer dissatisfaction, because that energy can't be contained. Many studies and reviews have drawn a direct link between employee satisfaction and turnover and customer satisfaction. People want to feel good. They do. They want to feel good, and they want to feel like they're doing good business. Even more importantly, they want to feel like they're doing good business with good people. They don't want to feel like the person who just delivered their package is going off and suffering, being demoralized, and not being cared for. I understand there are some people who don't care, and there are many who also ignore how they feel about this. But when surveyed, most people reported that they wanted the businesses they supported to have value systems that mattered.

I have this weirdly idealistic faith in humanity. I say "weird" because I honestly am not always sure what drives it when so much of what's out there seems bleak and disheartening. I don't deny the pain and struggle, but I do believe that most humans want to bring humanity back, not just into business but into our whole lives. I think that some people see the damage that's happening with companies, and they want to find ways to make it better. But there are a lot of people who have been hurt, experienced trauma, or are simply just burnt out. When people lose their spirit, they also lose options and possibilities.

People are tired of applying what sometimes feels like tone-deaf or arbitrary solutions to serious, perpetual problems. Instead, let's delve into the heart of what is causing these issues. What are the cycles of these problems, and how can we start solving them from the inside out? Let's expect our leaders to participate in the process of healing Corporate America, to be connected and accountable to purpose, and not just delegate that need and responsibility downward. We need to believe in humanity's resources instead of just human resources. Where are our actual human resources in business? Where can we go to feel like humans, to not feel replaceable, to not feel like we're just bots? Considering what is happening with changes in business and technology, this particular fear is ever-present. Any time a new technology emerges, it creates a lot of fear because change brings more change and ambiguity and, with that, fear. But I believe that within any type of change like that, there's an enormous amount of opportunity. Leaders have the opportunity to alleviate certain stresses from people's lives and allow them, as employees or as the talent they bring into an organization, to vibrate higher. We can use technology to remove overly redundant tasks that ultimately aren't beneficial to humans. We need to reevaluate why we expect organizations to function at the level that they do.

Why do we have what feels like such arbitrary rules around how company culture must function or act? We've seen a lot of seemingly arbitrary rules shift. In some ways, they weren't arbitrary; they were designed to create bias and presented as requirements. But as we see shifts in how people are allowed to show up in corporate culture, more acceptance for different expressions of personal style emerges. These changes are examples of companies recognizing the need for a more human-centered approach. It no longer works to solve culture challenges by constantly recruiting outside of the organization because you're not able to retain staff and continually place people into a toxic situation. When you step back and align employee values with the company culture, you won't just retain more staff. You will also capture the intellectual capital, knowledge, investment, training, and education that's been put into that individual. Over time, these investments add up and pay back exponentially.

Blaming is another thing that will only divide us more. When we holistically examine these challenges and consider solutions that benefit not just our employees but also extend beyond our business, we begin to see the potential for our impact. We are sick from our jobs, and there's a lot of data that shows the pressure and stress of the way we work and the lack of boundaries we create for ourselves. With COVID and work from home, it's created even more questions about boundaries and "work-life" balance. In some ways, it created even more challenges because people had fewer boundaries. They could maybe be more flexible with how they set their own schedule, but they were also in this situation where now they're always at work because their work is right there with them.

We have to look at our own health and take agency over that as individuals, recognizing that even in an environment that is detrimental or feels like it might be creating disease for us, we are participating in that energetically. The extent to which we relinquish our own agency and fall out of alignment with our value system also contributes to our illness. We can't just externalize that responsibility and say it belongs to the organization because when we do that, we are giving up enormous personal power and options. We have to take that responsibility for ourselves.

Organizations need to invest more in healing their cultures and less in wellness programs. While the employee does bear personal responsibility for their own health, it is disingenuous for a company to create a cycle of illness and expect the employee to resolve it when the actual problem lies within the organizational culture. In reality, investing in a healing culture means that you're going to invest in the people in your organization who are driving the culture, and you're going to help those people be better leaders so that you can ultimately improve the culture from the top down. All the wellness programs in the world aren't going to solve a situation where you have a toxic leader continually pumping that low-vibration energy; it's simply not sustainable.

As organizations, we have to invest in healing and preparing our leaders. Think about it. We have a generation of burned-out, untrained managers. I think anytime something becomes a running joke, it's not funny. The running joke of the middle manager – the useless, the angry, the whatever fill-in-the-blank middle manager – is old and hasn't been funny for a long time. I think of the middle manager as someone who is being crushed from both sides. That's what I tend to think of when I consider a middle manager, someone who has not been given the resources or the skills they need to expand themselves or others. I believe that in most companies, it's a burnout position. It leads to burnout when we put people in positions where they are sort of stuck and not given any opportunity to grow. Our leaders are also burning out, even the good ones, and maybe especially the good ones because there's so much working against them at a cultural level. People are dissatisfied. People are vocalizing their dissatisfaction, both customers and employees. They have a sense of less control. We've seen massive strikes, massive walkouts happening, and the expectations are high, and the stakes are really high. And we see leaders burn out.

On average, a CEO stays with an organization for less than ten years, with nearly 50% leaving in less than five years.[60] When you consider the impact that leadership has on culture, that type of change can damage an organization. One example of this is Southwest Airlines. Since their inception, they have promoted and expressed a culture centered around the idea of "people first" values that were often expressed with frugality and fun. That's how I would sum it up. Co-founder Herb Kelleher was invested in these values, and he infused them into the culture. He was an active force of nature in his business, and for many years of my life, I flew Southwest. Some of the most enjoyable in-air experiences of my life happened on Southwest planes because of that culture of fun and experience it created. The people who worked there seemed to love their jobs and it made the whole experience better.

Mr. Kelleher passed away in 2019, holding Emeritus Chairman status. But, I think many people noticed there was a clear shift in the culture at the time he became less directly involved. In 2022, this culminated in chaos during an exceptionally challenging holiday travel season, and Southwest found their unique culture in jeopardy.[61] Howard was a committed CEO who was recognized for his leadership, influence, and "Employees First" approach. In many ways, this energy may be hard for some organizations to capture. How do you take someone's charisma and core values and infuse them into a legacy? This is part of the question we can explore when we consider how and where business culture needs to shift. Just like with Boeing in recent years, we've seen Southwest take some hits to their brand, but they have been able to navigate this better because of the core values built into their culture and

---

[60] Jerotich, Carol, and Joyce Chen. "CEO Tenure Rates." *The Harvard Law School Forum on Corporate Governance*, 4 Aug. 2023, corpgov.law.harvard.edu/2023/08/04/ceo-tenure-rates-2/#:~:text=The%20data%20reveals%2039%25%20of.

[61] Couch, Michael. "Council Post: Organizational Culture Lessons You Can Learn from Southwest Airlines' Debacle." Forbes, www.forbes.com/sites/forbescoachescouncil/2023/02/24/organizational-culture-lessons-you-can-learn-from-southwest-airlines-debacle/?sh=5f75d12c4684.

then continued alignment to those values. When the values are so completely misaligned, it becomes much more difficult for organizations to recover from these types of scenarios.

Action Items and Journal Prompts: Chapter 11

Reflections

- Do you follow any arbitrary rules in your own life? Habits or rituals that you inherited and have possibly outgrown.

- Take time to examine the intention behind your daily rituals and the "rules" you have for yourself. Make a list of them. Do they help you move forward or hold you in place?

- Have you ever felt betrayed by a brand? Did you continue to support that brand? Describe your feelings and what made you shift your perspective.

- Do you feel like your company imposes arbitrary rules? If yes, do you believe they help or impede the culture or productivity in your environment?

- If you could change or implement a rule at work, what would it be and why would you change it?

Actions

- **Break a Rule.** Choose one arbitrary rule you have for yourself that is holding you back. Break the rule and see what changes for you. We're taught not to break rules. Examine how it feels and what you learn about yourself.

  Examples:

  - You always let others speak first - this time, speak first.
  - You say please when making a request - be polite, but eliminate the "please."

- You never take a break - take it and model self-care for others.

These are just examples. The point is to create your own personal culture shift.

- **Explore the World Around You**. Engage in a new cultural experience with a curious, learning mind. Allow yourself to be completely present in the experience, without judgment, with the goal of expanding your understanding and personal perspective. Alternatively, share something about your culture with someone else.

CHAPTER 12

LEADERS AT EVERY LEVEL

"First be a leader of yourself. Only then can you grow to lead others."
– David Taylor-Klaus, Entrepreneur, Author, and Executive Coach

You Leading You

Essentially, leading at every level is about leading yourself first. In this way, people can lead from wherever they are, regardless of their title or position. It doesn't matter if you are in the lowest entry-level position of an organization, a brand-new role that you just started, a middle management position, or if you're a full-blown owner or executive. Whatever role you play in an organization, or frankly, as an individual in life, you have the capacity to lead, and there are things you can do to access leadership energy. The best place to begin is with awareness of your energy, emotions, and behavior. A lot of people have experienced unresolved, sometimes unacknowledged trauma. I don't think that trauma is necessarily something that is unique or exclusive in a general sense, but I believe that every individual's trauma is deeply unique, personal, and an experience that only they can know. Our ability or capacity to work through that trauma can have a huge impact on how our life plays out when it comes to our emotional awareness and our emotional reactivity. Unresolved trauma can generate a lot of challenges and chaos in a person's life.

I experienced trauma very early in childhood, and it wasn't diagnosed until my middle-aged adulthood. In the intervening years, I was on a trauma-healing journey, trying to comprehend patterns in my life that I was aware of but didn't fully understand what was causing them. It was through seeking therapy and other mindfulness practices that I was able to get to a point where I could process the trauma, not just process it but have complete and total awareness of it, and process it in a way that I was no longer reliving those experiences, and it no longer controlled my life. As I was able to do that, it allowed me to engage in shadow work.

Carl Jung, the psychologist, introduced the concept of the shadow in the human psyche. Basically, by shadow, we simply mean what is unseen. The unseen refers to experiences and situations that create protective emotions and behaviors. This includes things we learn to express and things we also repress. What we repress is placed in our shadow, and on a conscious level, we continue to push it away. If we have unresolved trauma or issues that require therapy, it's very difficult to do shadow work because shadow work requires a certain level of emotional awareness and intelligence to delve into the unconscious psyche and understand more about what drives our emotional and physical behaviors. When we haven't processed trauma, our defense mechanisms are strong and are difficult to break through, as they protect us from our shadow. As you engage in shadow work and start working with the persona and the shadow, it allows for self-integration. This leads to whole self-integration where you're taking both logos and pathos, the feeling and the logic, and integrating them. You develop stronger intuition and learn to trust your instincts. For me, this has been a process throughout my life, and it will be a lifelong journey. Personal growth is a lifelong process for everyone, but we all have different experiences. I have met people, both younger and older than me, who have achieved enough self-integration to offer valuable insights. This is why I believe we can learn from each other at every level and why we shouldn't dismiss people with sweeping generalizations.

Another aspect of being able to lead from wherever you are is activating your personal values and being proactive with them. Honoring your values makes it much easier to make decisions in life. You're able to quickly assess situations.

If you've done the spiritual work to understand your value systems and how they impact your purpose and what you're working towards in life, then honoring those values becomes very easy. Even when they shift, you recognize that more quickly. For example, you may notice that something once important to you like socializing and hanging out with friends, might give way to valuing personal time, family, and being more connected to your home. This value shift happens, and it's not about judging either value as better or worse but acknowledging that each value served your needs at the time. Honoring the value is what's important. As you know yourself more and understand yourself more in these ways, you truly learn to lead from within. You're able to express leadership in any situation.

So, what does leading from within really look like? It's not about externalizing problems. Leading from within is about taking accountability first. It involves acknowledging the role you play and the energy you contribute to a situation. You don't show up as a victim but in a space of personal agency and empowerment. You refrain from blaming and understand what's within your control, being present and able to assess situations without judging them as good or bad. Intuitively, you'll know when to speak up with authority and offer guidance or when to be a team player and offer support. Leading doesn't always express itself as obvious authority; sometimes, it's simply modeling behavior that creates more harmony or productivity in an environment.

Leading from within means having a connection to both your conscious and unconscious mind and developing a level of emotional responsiveness where you're less triggered by others and situations, allowing you to take a moment to assess and then respond in the way you wish. I encourage people to become the leaders they wish they had. People often externalize, complaining about their boss's actions or lack of recognition. While it may be true that you can't control your boss's behavior, how you respond and engage with it significantly influences the outcome. Modeling the behavior you wish to see is always the first step towards honoring yourself. If you find yourself wishing your boss acted differently, the first question to ask is whether you're embodying that behavior yourself.

Paying attention to leaders who are doing it right, learning from them, and being willing to evaluate your own approach, skills, and awareness are crucial steps. Look at how other leaders have stepped into their roles, embraced authority, expressed empathy, and inspired those around them. Most importantly, be willing to expand your thinking. True leaders are always gathering information from everything around them, including themselves. They assess the flow, harmony, disruption, chaos, and even the silence – what's not being said or seen. They're taking all of that information and learning from it. They use what they learn, test it, and they may fail or succeed. Regardless, they continue to learn, refine, expand, and, most importantly, teach.

Organizations Leveling Up

Organizations and business leaders can also promote leaders at every level by nurturing a culture that values respect, integrity, communication, and trust. We have made leadership so much about the hierarchy that we have, in many ways, lost our ability to ascend. Businesses need to assess leadership objectively and then invest in development and growth that will go beyond just enhancing one individual's career path toward having a profound impact on the culture. The ROI for investing in good leadership should include retention and less employee dissatisfaction.

Throughout my career, I have attended several management training classes. As an employee and manager, I have been required to take training courses on how to avoid certain types of workplace behavior, such as harassment or bullying. As I took in the information, I remember several times wondering why we were always telling people what they shouldn't do rather than giving them the skills to do better. It felt like such a waste of time, or an exercise meant to check off a box. The people who needed this training the most wouldn't pay attention to it. Instead of investing in managing these issues, organizations should invest in measuring emotional intelligence along with skills and other requirements for a position. Training human resources and business leaders to be emotionally responsive and ascertain the emotional skills of another person allows an organization to bring in and develop someone at any level.

According to *Forbes*, three key styles of leadership will be most effective in 2024. These are: **adaptive, inclusive, and transformational**.[62] All of these styles are dependent on a balance of skills but are especially enhanced with emotional intelligence. Investing in leadership development while also considering how companies themselves can exhibit these qualities will be crucial to sustainable success and growth. Companies can lead from within their industries with a willingness to drive changes to enact real change and set newer, better standards for how business is done. Companies that are willing to adopt adaptable business practices that prioritize inclusivity and offer transformational solutions for their customers and transformational growth experiences for their employees will edge out those that stubbornly hold onto tired processes.

---

[62] Wells, Rachel. "3 Leadership Styles of Highly Effective Leaders in 2024." Forbes, www.forbes.com/sites/rachelwells/2024/02/11/3-leadership-styles-of-highly-effective-leaders-in-2024/?sh=60b02dc262db.

The Future of Leadership and Business

First, I am optimistic; it's in my nature to be that way, but I also see things that reinforce my optimism. Sometimes, I feel alone in this perspective. I feel like every time I say I'm optimistic, I make people angry. If so, I apologize to all the people out there that I've just angered with my optimism, but I believe that people are becoming hyper-aware of the cost and the unsustainability of toxic culture and poor leadership. I think we will see more businesses actively invest in solving this issue by preparing their leaders and managers for the roles, responsibilities, and expectations placed on them. I believe businesses will recognize that there is a financial return in emphasizing and activating values personally and professionally. The ROI will show up with less employee turnover, combined with more loyalty and trust, creating real environments and cultures that are built around respect, honoring individuals' needs, and the purpose of the business itself.

I also think that we are witnessing an explosion in entrepreneurship. Recent studies show that over 45%, almost 50% of individuals polled, cited complete dissatisfaction with Corporate America. In that same study, 35% to 50% of the people polled said they would be self-employed within two years.[63] This trend was higher among younger and highly educated people. But even on the lower end, the 35%, which was an average of not necessarily younger or highly educated, indicates that people are looking at being their own boss, starting their own businesses, and leading themselves. Depending on how companies and organizations view this, it represents more competition for them and fewer employee resources. It could impact Corporate America, and it is already having an effect.

---

[63] Isador, Graham. "20 Surprising Entrepreneur Statistics to Know in 2023." *NorthOne*, www.northone.com/blog/small-business/entrepreneur-statistics.

I think we're going to see more alignment of profit and purpose. And we can ask, is that even possible? But I think in some cases, it might be required because, if we look at the data of what customers are expecting right now, they are expecting companies to live up to their values. I believe that when companies are more value-aligned, what we're going to see are more value-aligned investment opportunities. We've already seen this happen in some industries, such as the cannabis industry, which is turbulent and interesting in relation to legalities, laws, and the clash between populist needs and wants versus various state laws and federal laws affecting banking. We've seen some investment groups start up just to support this industry. There is potential for cannabis to be rescheduled from a Schedule I to a Schedule III drug, and should this occur, the opportunities for investing in this industry are predicted to expand significantly.[64] I believe there are other investment groups focused on supporting very specific causes, industries, or actions they wish to elevate and see as well-supported. This concept is likely to continue expanding, with more investments related to businesses that align with the values investors are focusing on. I am a cheerleader for the idea that companies will vibrate at a higher frequency, embodying progressive-minded business practices, but I am pragmatic enough to understand that money and profit are driving forces in business.

Companies are exploring how to align their values by implementing hybrid benefit solutions and creating true value-activated programs. I believe progressive corporate culture will be the future of business and hope this happens through great collaboration. Organizations clinging to outdated methods, resistant to change or evolution, will fall behind and become relics in the history of corporate evolution. While my predictions may seem mystic, it is my highest hope they come true. Corporate traumatic stress disorder is a real issue, with many individuals harmed by the existing system. Yet, I believe

---

[64] "Cannabis Predictions for 2024." Benesch, Friedlander, Coplan & Aronoff LLP - Cannabis Predictions for 2024, www.beneschlaw.com/resources/cannabis-predictions-for-2024.html.

this system is worth saving and evolving, for it holds considerable value. Impermanence is a fundamental aspect of life; nothing is meant to stay the same without change. This applies to people as well as businesses and systems.

Action Items and Journal Prompts: Chapter 12

Reflections

- Think back to a moment in your life when you "took charge." What was happening or what compelled you to take action? How did you feel?

- Are there situations where you feel more or less confident expressing yourself as a leader? What can you learn about yourself by examining these experiences?

- Have you witnessed another person stepping into a leadership role, even when they weren't the designated leader? What did you notice about their energy? Did it seem courageous or egotistical? Examine your feelings in this experience.

- How is leadership approached in your organization? Do you think your leaders are connected to employee and customer experiences? How could they improve?

- What is one value that you wish your company would express with clarity? What actions could your company take to make that happen? Are there any actions you can take?

Actions

- **Expand Your Skills.** Whether you're a seasoned leader or just getting started, objectivity and insight are cornerstones of great leaders. If you are leading or if you want to lead more - make sure you have a trusted advisor, coach, or mentor. Our egos can easily get in the way of our progress. Find a partner in your development and do the work. Leadership, like meditation, is a practice of infinite transformation.

- **Lead Something.** Maybe you're not a leader at work... yet. But, as I just mentioned, leadership takes practice, and there are plenty of places to begin. Start a group in your community. Volunteer for a committee position. Lead your neighborhood in a trash cleanup. Be willing to step into leadership roles and assume the responsibility that comes with it.

ONE LAST THOUGHT

Thank you for taking this journey with me. I am sure, at times, you were traveling, uncertain where we would end up, and I appreciate your trust in me and your willingness to explore. My goal was to examine the influence of toxic culture on the individual and the organization. As individuals, we know we have shadows, and I believe in *Brand Shadows* too. It is an inextricable relationship we have with the work we do and who we are doing it for, or who is doing it for us. We all participate in this dance, sometimes with confidence and enthusiasm, and sometimes we feel paralyzed with fear, or puppeteered without control.

These days, when I talk with people, I hear much more fear than enthusiasm. For a long time, I think businesses could ignore this and just maintain the status quo, but I don't think that's true anymore. Things are changing and they need to. I love business, and I love people. I really believe there is a space for us to evolve forward, and it begins with looking inward and having a willingness to grow and expand our perspective of what is possible.

I hope you found something in this that inspires you to take a risk, speak up, empower yourself, and improve your environment. If you're a leader who impacts many, I hope you do all of that on behalf of your organization. Take a risk and reveal your *Brand Shadow*. Speak up and be transparent about your organizational values. Empower yourself to make changes and grow as a leader. Improve your environment by proactively healing your culture in honest and authentic ways.

Nothing ever has to "be that way" just because it's always "been that way."

With joy,
Stephanie Crain
Corporate Mystic

THANK YOU FOR READING MY BOOK!

Thank you for reading my book! Here are a few free bonus resources.

Scan the QR Code:

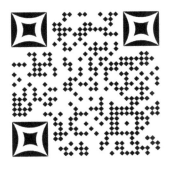

I appreciate your interest in my book and value your feedback as it helps me improve future versions of this book. I would appreciate it if you could leave your invaluable review on Amazon.com with your feedback. Thank you!

SOURCES

1. Adams, Chris. "Do Our Customers Really Care about Corporate Values?" LinkedIn, 7 Aug. 2018, www.linkedin.com/pulse/do-our-customers-really-care-corporate-values-chris-adams/.

2. Asare, Janice Gassam. "How Hair Discrimination Affects Black Women at Work." Harvard Business Review, 10 May 2023, hbr.org/2023/05/how-hair-discrimination-affects-black-women-at-work.

3. Bivens, Josh, and Jori Kandra. "CEO Pay Has Skyrocketed 1,460% since 1978: CEOs Were Paid 399 Times as Much as a Typical Worker in 2021." Economic Policy Institute, 4 Oct. 2022, www.epi.org/publication/ceo-pay-in-2021/.

4. Boyd, Danielle. "Workplace Stress." The American Institute of Stress, 2022, www.stress.org/workplace-stress#:~:text=83%25%20of%20US%20workers%20suffer.

5. Brecheisen, J. "Perception of Mental Health at Work." Gallup, 3 Aug. 2023, www.gallup.com/workplace/508622/perception-mental-health-work.aspx#:~:text=HR%20Professionals%20and%20U.S.%20Workforce%20Insights&text=Among%20HR%20professionals%2C%2035%25%20reported,challenges%20in%20their%20own%20role.

6. Brower, T. "Managers Have Major Impact on Mental Health: How to Lead for Wellbeing." Forbes, 29 Jan. 2023, www.forbes.com/sites/tracybrower/2023/01/29/managers-have-major-impact-on-mental-health-how-to-lead-for-wellbeing/?sh=6e038ec92ec1.

44476765554566765565764435564345566555

7. Campbell, L. "Half of HR Managers Consider Quitting Due to Pressure of Mental Health Crisis." The HR Director, 3 Feb. 2023, www.thehrdirector.com/business-news-mental-health/half-of-hr-managers-consider-quitting-due-to-pressure-of-mental-health-crisis/.

8. Clayton, Neil Barman and Sarah Jensen. "The Chief Culture Officer Role Is Quickly Disappearing." Quartz, 31 Aug. 2023, qz.com/the-chief-culture-officer-role-is-quickly-disappearing-1850789015.

9. Couch, Michael. "Council Post: Organizational Culture Lessons You Can Learn from Southwest Airlines' Debacle." Forbes, www.forbes.com/sites/forbescoachescouncil/2023/02/24/organizational-culture-lessons-you-can-learn-from-southwest-airlines-debacle/?sh=5f75d12c4684.

10. Davis, Kathleen. "9 Workplace Trends for 2024 That Will Change Our Work Lives." Fast Company, Fast Company, 26 Jan. 2024, fastcompany.com/91016529/9-workplace-trends-for-2024-that-will-change-our-work-lives.

11. Dobbin, Frank, and Alexandra Kalev. "Why Diversity Programs Fail." Harvard Business Review, July–Aug. 2016, hbr.org/2016/07/why-diversity-programs-fail.

12. Dumont, Marvin. "4 Biggest Merger and Acquisition Disasters." Investopedia, 21 Feb. 2022, investopedia.com/articles/financial-theory/08/merger-acquisition-disasters.asp.

13. Fickman, Laurie. "The Job You Want vs. the Job You Get." University of Houston, uh.edu/news-events/stories/2021/june-2021/06242021-dream-job-not-reality-kevin-hoff.php.

14. Gleeson, Brent. "The Top 5 Leadership Trends That Will Drive Success in 2024." Forbes, 2 Jan. 2024, www.forbes.com/sites/brentgleeson/2024/01/02/the-top-5-leadership-trends-that-will-drive-success-in-2024/?sh=77367ba23da0.

15. Goldman Sachs. "The Recent Emergence of Generative Artificial Intelligence (AI) Raises Whether We." 26 Mar. 2023, https://www.goldmansachs.com/intelligence/topics/artificial-intelligence.html#:~:text=.

16. Green, Jeff, et al. "Corporate America Promised to Hire a Lot More People of Color. It Actually Did." Bloomberg.com, 25 Sept. 2023, www.bloomberg.com/graphics/2023

    1. -black-lives-matter-equal-opportunity-corporate-diversity/.

17. Harmon, A. "Why Multiple Companies Aren't Requiring College Degrees Anymore." Recruiter.com, www.recruiter.com/recruiting/why-multiple-companies-arent-requiring-college-degrees-anymore/.

18. Harmon, K. "Suicide Rates for 2023 at an All-Time High for the United States." WPMI, 4 Jan. 2024, mynbc15.com/news/nation-world/suicide-rates-for-2023-at-an-all-time-high-for-the-united-states.

19. Hansen, Megan. "Who Benefits from the Gig Economy?" James Madison Institute, 14 Mar. 2019, jamesmadison.org/who-benefits-from-the-gig-economy/.

20. Hanson, Melanie. "Average Student Loan Debt." EducationData.org, 22 May 2023, educationdata.org/average-student-loan-debt#:~:text=The%20average%20federal%20student%20loan.

21. Heilferty, Annarose. "CHRO Trends 2022 Report." The Talent Strategy Group, 13 July 2022, talentstrategygroup.com/chro-trends-2022-report/#:~:text=In%20total%2C%20187%20of%20the.

22. Heinz, Kate, and Brennan Whitfield. "38 Employee Turnover Statistics to Know." Built In, 17 Apr. 2023, builtin.com/recruiting/employee-turnover-statistics.

23. "Highest Suicide Rate by Profession." Joshua York Foundation, www.joshuayorkfoundation.org/blog/highest-suicide-rate-by-profession/.

24. Horch, AJ. "The Days of Elaborate Corporate Perks Are Now behind Us." Nasdaq, 24 Jan. 2023, www.nasdaq.com/articles/the-days-of-elaborate-corporate-perks-are-now-behind-us.

25. Hougaard, R. and Jacqueline Carter, "Ego Is the Enemy of Good Leadership." Harvard Business Review, 6 Nov. 2018, hbr.org/2018/11/ego-is-the-enemy-of-good-leadership.

26. Howe, Amy. "Supreme Court Strikes Down Affirmative Action Programs in College Admissions." SCOTUSblog, 29 June 2023, www.scotusblog.com/2023/06/supreme-court-strikes-down-affirmative-action-programs-in-college-admissions/.

27. Jay, Shani. "13 Tried-And-Tested DEI Initiatives to Implement [in 2023]." AIHR, 17 July 2023, www.aihr.com/blog/dei-initiatives/.

28. JP. "NACAC College Admission Process Survey." National Association for College Admission Counseling (NACAC), 22 Aug. 2023, www.nacacnet.org/nacac-college-admission-process-survey/.

29. Kenny, Graham. "Don't Make This Common M&A Mistake." Harvard Business Review, 16 Mar. 2020, hbr.org/2020/03/don't-make-this-common-ma-mistake.

30. Kirschner, Kylie. "Microsoft CEO Satya Nadella Says Empathy Isn't a Soft Skill – It's Actually 'the Hardest Skill We Learn'." Business Insider, Sep. 2023, www.businessinsider.com/microsoft-ceo-satya-nadella-empathy-hard-not-soft-skill-2023-10.

31. Marcus, Jon. "How Higher Education Lost Its Shine." The Hechinger Report, 10 Aug. 2022, https://hechingerreport.org/how-higher-education-lost-its-shine/.

32. Marken, Stephanie. "A Crisis in Confidence in Higher Ed." Gallup, 12 Apr. 2019, https://news.gallup.com/opinion/gallup/248492/crisis-confidence-higher.aspx.

33. Marr, Bernard. "9 Workplace Trends for 2024 That Will Change Our Work Lives." Fast Company, 28 Dec. 2023, www.fastcompany.com/91016529/9-workplace-trends-for-2024-that-will-change-our-work-lives.

34. Marr, Bernard. "New Report Finds Growth of Women Business Owners Outpaces the Market." Wells Fargo Newsroom, 9 Jan. 2024, https://newsroom.wf.com/English/news-releases/news-release-details/2024/New-Report-Finds-Growth-of-Women-Business-Owners-Outpaces-the-Market/.

35. Mayer, K. "SHRM Research: Work Negatively Impacting Employees' Mental Health." SHRM, 1 May 2023, www.shrm.org/topics-tools/news/benefits-compensation/shrm-research-work-negatively-impacting-employees-mental-health.

36. McFeely, Shane, and Ben Wigert. "This Fixable Problem Costs U.S. Businesses $1 Trillion." Gallup, 13 Mar. 2019, www.gallup.com/workplace/247391/fixable-problem-costs-businesses-trillion.aspx.

37. Michels, David. "Now Is Not The Time To Give Up On DEI." Forbes, 26 May 2023, forbes.com/sites/davidmichels/2023/05/26/now-is-not-the-time-to-give-up-on-dei/?sh=1025f9f85121.

38. Minvielle, Luis. "The Glassdoor Dilemma: Unveiling the Truth Behind Company Reviews." We Are Developers, 14 July 2023, www.wearedevelopers.com/magazine/does-glassdoor-remove-negative-company-reviews.

39. Morris, Chris. "The Days of Elaborate Corporate Perks Are Now Behind Us." Nasdaq, 11 May 2023, nasdaq.com/articles/the-days-of-elaborate-corporate-perks-are-now-behind-us.

40. Murphy, Mark. "A Shocking Number of Leaders Are Not Aligned with Their Companies' Visions." Forbes, 28 Aug. 2020, www.forbes.com/sites/markmurphy/2020/08/28/a-shocking-number-of-leaders-are-not-aligned-with-their-companies-visions/?sh=3bcacfb41acf.

41. Nicola, Tara P. "Majority of Gen Z Consider College Education Important." Gallup, 14 Sept. 2023, https://news.gallup.com/opinion/gallup/509906/majority-gen-consider-college-education-important.aspx.

42. Peavler, Rosemary. "The Demise of the Defined-Benefit Plan." Investopedia, 17 Aug. 2022, www.investopedia.com/articles/retirement/06/demiseofdbplan.asp.

43. Peck. E. "Companies Are Backing Away from 'DEI'." Axios, 4 Jan. 2024, https://www.axios.com/2024/01/04/dei-jobs-diversity-corporate.

44. Pollman, E. "Startup Failure." The Harvard Law School Forum on Corporate Governance, 29 Sept. 2023, corpgov.law.harvard.edu/2023/09/29/startup-failure/#:~:text=This%20can%20occur%20for%20a,market%20need%2C%20or%20changed%20circumstances.

45. Press, Gil. "Generative AI and The Future of Creative Jobs." Forbes, 6 Mar. 2023, https://www.forbes.com/sites/gilpress/2023/03/06/generative-ai-and-the-future-of-creative-jobs/?sh=d310b516617a.

46. "Purpose and Shareholder Value: Have Your Cake and Eat It, Too." Chief Executive, https://chiefexecutive.net/purpose-and-shareholder-value-have-your-cake-and-eat-it-too/

47. "Reveal Your Community of Experience," DRG, https://www.thedrg.com/integrating-cx-and-ex/#:~:text=Company%20culture%20must%20be%20fueled,do%20you%20make%20it%20happen%3F

48. Ryan, Liz. "Ten Signs Of A Progressive Company Culture." Forbes, 14 Mar. 2016, forbes.com/sites/lizryan/2016/03/14/ten-signs-of-a-progressive-company-culture/?sh=7b52caf77382.

49. Schaeffer, Katherine. "Striking Findings from 2023." Pew Research Center, 8 Dec. 2023, https://www.pewresearch.org/short-reads/2023/12/08/striking-findings-from-2023/.

50. Shefrin, Hersh. "Boeing's Weak Corporate Culture Underlies Difficulties With 737 MAX 9." Forbes, 28 Jan. 2024,

forbes.com/sites/hershshefrin/2024/01/28/boeings-weak-corporate-culture-underlies-difficulties-with-737-max-9/?sh=7c57ddb0a695.

51. Sickler, Jonas. "How to Remove Negative Glassdoor Reviews."ReputationManagement.com, 10 Oct. 2019, updated 22 Oct. 2019, www.reputationmanagement.com/blog/remove-glassdoor-reviews/.

52. Smith, Greg. "Council Post: Core Values Can Supercharge Your Creator Business: Here's How." Forbes, 24 Aug. 2023, www.forbes.com/sites/forbestechcouncil/2023/08/24/core-values-can-supercharge-your-creator-business-heres-how/?sh=523192f53f82.

53. Soutar, L. "'Real Implications': Huge Majority of HR Leaders Agree D&I Crucial for Business Performance." HR Grapevine, 10 Aug. 2023, https://www.hrgrapevine.com/content/article/2023-08-09-huge-majority-of-hr-leaders-agree-di-crucial-for-business-performance

54. "Stack Overflow Developer Survey 2023." Stack Overflow, 2023, survey.stackoverflow.co/2023/.

55. Syme, Pete. "Boeing's Quality-Control Process and Company Culture Are Being Heavily Scrutinized after the 737 Max Flight 1282 Blowout." Business Insider, Jan. 2024, www.businessinsider.com/boeing-737-max-quality-control-company-culture-merger-finances-2024-1#.

56. Taylor, Kate. "College Admissions Scandal." The New York Times, 8 Oct. 2019, www.nytimes.com/news-event/college-admissions-scandal.

57. TeamStage, "Tattoos in the Workplace Statistics in 2022." TeamStage, 13 Apr. 2022, teamstage.io/tattoos-in-the-workplace-statistics/.

58. Thakor, Anjan. "Purpose and Shareholder Value: Have Your Cake and Eat It Too." Chief Executive, 2 July 2022, chiefexecutive.net/purpose-and-shareholder-value-have-your-cake-and-eat-it-too/.

59. Torkington, S. "How Might Generative AI Change Creative Jobs?" World Economic Forum, 9 May 2023, https://www.weforum.org/agenda/2023/05/generative-ai-creative-jobs/

60. "Toxic Workplace Cultures Cost Companies Billions." DaMar Staffing Solutions of Indianapolis, 8 Feb. 2023, www.damarstaff.com/blog-posting/2023/2/8/toxic-workplace-cultures-cost-companies-billions#:~:text=One%20in%20five%20Americans%20has.

61. "Walmart's Latest Perk for U.S. Store Managers: Stock Grants." ABC27, 29 Jan. 2024, abc27.com/news/us-world/business/ap-walmarts-latest-perk-for-u-s-store-managers-stock-grants/.

62. Wang, Ying, et al. "Employee Perceptions of HR Practices: A Critical Review and Future Directions." The International Journal of Human Resource Management, vol. 31, no. 1, 26 Nov. 2019, pp. 128–173, https://doi.org/10.1080/09585192.2019.1674360.

63. Wells, Rachel. "3 Leadership Styles of Highly Effective Leaders in 2024." Forbes, www.forbes.com/sites/rachelwells/2024/02/11/3-leadership-styles-of-highly-effective-leaders-in-2024/?sh=60b02dc262db.

64. White, Martha C. "The Pension: That Rare Retirement Benefit Gets a Fresh Look." The New York Times, 24 Nov. 2023, https://www.nytimes.com/2023/11/24/business/pension-retirement.html

65. Whitfield, Dawson. "Top 4 Reasons Employees Don't Believe in Your Mission, Vision, and Values (And What to Do About It)." 6Q, 22 July

2020, inside.6q.io/employees-don't-believe-in-your-mission-vision-and-values/.

66. "Who Benefits from the Gig Economy?" JamesJames Madison Institute, 14 Mar. 2019, jamesmadison.org/who-benefits-from-the-gig-economy/.